BE FRUSTRATED
BE TERRIFIED
BE HEARTBROKEN

A CONVERSATION ON THE SUBJECT OF CULTIVATING A LIFE WORTH LIVING

JASON D. TUZINKEWICH

Jason D. Tuzinkewich/Be Frustrated, Be Terrified, Be Heartbroken
Printed in the United States of America

Be Frustrated, Be Terrified, Be Heartbroken/Jason D. Tuzinkewich. -- 1st ed.

ISBN 978-0-9976346-0-0 Print Edition
ISBN 978-0-9976346-1-7 Ebook Edition

Table of Contents

Acknowledgements:

There are so many people who touch our lives and help to shape who we grow to be, and how we view the world at large. A well-placed smile or misdirected anger can so often change the course of a day, and impact the development of perceptions. For these reasons, it is impossible to adequately acknowledge everyone who has impacted the writing of this book by name. If we have shared any time together, you can rest assured that you are a part of this text. Whether our acquaintance was positive, or produced learning through challenges poorly navigated, I thank you with deepest sincerity for helping me to learn and grow. If you recognize your hand in the stories and lessons of the text, I would love to hear from you, and invite you to reach out to me via one of the contact channels at the end of the book.

There are a few people who warrant direct acknowledgement by name. My book team: Corey, Mark and Colin, thank you so very much! You have made this a truly special journey, and because of you, I believe that we have created something meaningful. My village: Amber, Craig, Ruth, the Wilde family, the Stone family, the Van Laanen family, Mr. Guerlain, Wild Bill, Eric, Michael, and everyone who has shared so very much love and support throughout my journey, I thank you with all my heart. I know what it is like to feel as though you don't have a village, and that makes me love and appreciate you that much more. I know that I have not always been the greatest friend, brother, uncle or partner, and I thank you for loving me enough to call me out, carry me, and celebrate with me when each was warranted. I thank you for trusting me enough that I could do the same for you. To everyone I am not in touch with, but who shared pieces of your journey with me: know that you are a part of who I am. Many of you I think of often, and I wish you a fruitful and fulfilling life.

Preface

Let me begin by telling you openly that the original working title for this book was *Be Fearless, Be Focused, Be Loved.*

In reflecting on the journey of my life and the message I wanted to convey, I realized that a title like that is a part of the problem I'm attempting to address. Setting lofty goals for outcomes that you have no control over is one of the obstacles that often make life feel so difficult in the first place. I don't want to add to the burdens that limit your happiness. Rather, my intention is to have a discussion that shares some of the lessons I have learned in the hope that they open new doors in your journey.

Here is one frightening truth you probably already suspect: You're going to have to face your demons to find your happiness.

I am not going to lie to you, and I challenge you not to lie to yourself. Life can be a struggle. We don't always get what we want. Or we achieve our goals and they fail to make us happy. My own story is filled with victories and failures too numerous to count. I have heard advice from every person willing to add his or her two cents. I have studied the people in my life that I admire and have read scores of books on philosophy, living, leadership, and the like. Some of this advice I was able to abide by. Some didn't resonate with me. Some was simply too challenging for me at the time. What struck me the most was how all of these varied and, I am certain, well-meaning sources had one thing in common: the rejection of the negative. *You've got to accentuate the positive, eliminate the negative...* Isn't that how the Bing Crosby song goes?

With all due respect to Bing, I disagree. I propose that a paradigm shift is necessary in order to achieve true fulfillment.

——————

Rather than attempting to deny the inevitable hardships and failures, the warts and the missteps we all experience, we must prepare ourselves to accept them. Face them head on and turn them into springboards for all the good we expect to achieve in our lives.

——————

This book is intended to present an honest, objective, and realistic outlook on how to mentally prepare yourself to deal with hardship and turmoil.

Only in this way can you maximize the happiness, success, and love in your life.

Happiness, success, and love... Aren't those three critical elements you think of having when you envision a "life worth living"?

First off, let's define the real goal. What does a "life worth living" look like for you? Let me save you some time in this process. Although you will likely spend the rest of your days on earth answering this question anew, in the early stages your response may change every single day. That's okay. Shifting goals and priorities are often a signal that environment is playing a part in the process. It's not unusual or undesirable to be influenced—at least some of the time—by what society or your family or your friends want from you. But that formula of achieving only the goals other people set for you is how so many adults find themselves completely unfulfilled by their lives.

Career, friends and family, and coveted possessions only get you so far. You are the only person who can decide what will make you deeply happy. The more you try to answer that question, the more easily you will be able to eliminate the things that don't actually matter. Once that clutter is cleared away, your true purpose emerges. A well-honed definition of a worthwhile life is as complete as it is simple. It applies universally to every facet of your life. Maybe it is service to others. Maybe it is expression of your creativity. Maybe it is solving a scientific problem. Purpose is derived from an individual's talents and tendencies. It is made of the stuff you dream about and long for.

Arriving at your own ideal life goal is wildly satisfying. From that fixed point, you can make decisions with confidence. You can create a legacy that will define how others view you and how you will impact the world around you. Defining what "a life worth living" means to you, and being true to it, will be the single most profound thing you will ever do. Understanding the implications of this definition and how to apply the lessons of living it every moment of every day will be a lifelong process. You will, no doubt, see positive effects immediately. Though it takes a short time to learn all the principles, a lifetime is required to master their nuance in action. You will need to be vigilant. Never stop asking questions and demanding that you answer them honestly.

The hard truth is that we will all fail, experience loss, and feel deep personal pain. To deny these truths only makes their occurrence that much more devastating. That's why I titled the book *Be Frustrated, Be Terrified, Be Heartbroken.*

I truly believe that life is little more than an opportunity to become the best person we can possibly be. That journey is how we find joy. We don't arrive at success and then experience contentment for the rest of our days, blissfully coasting along on our laurels. Instead, through effort, we become better, stronger, more truthful people and the result of that effort (and the service it can provide for others) IS happiness. Self-reliance IS success. Sharing life's moments with our special people IS love.

In my career thus far, I've been fortunate to be a chemical engineer, a cordon bleu accredited chef, a sought-after restaurant consultant, a pioneer in alternative fuel technology and, most recently, a mergers and acquisitions advisor. I'm one of those driven, curious people whose thirst for knowledge knows no bounds. My journey thus far has astounded me in its diversity. I have been blessed with many opportunities to succeed and have failed frequently.

In times when circumstances unraveled right before my eyes, I often thought, "I am not designed to succeed in this environment." It was terrifying. I believe that all of us have those moments. No matter what words we use to describe it, that feeling of discomfort, of unease makes us shiver and tense up. We think, "Everybody else seems to be navigating this just fine, why can't I?" That bewildered sensation is what got me writing this book in the first place. It's the question that permeates my life.

In this book, I have tried to lay out some tools that have worked for me. Tools for figuring out what happiness looks like by one's own definition. Tools for negotiating through obstacles. Tools for making decisions. It's my belief that we aren't really growing, changing, and developing as people if we don't put ourselves in places where we are at times frustrated, terrified, or heartbroken. When we're feeling those things, it doesn't mean that all is lost.

———

These emotions are indicators that we need to grow. Frustration, fear, and heartbreak are opportunities life is giving you for change. Heed them.

———

BOOK I

BE FRUSTRATED

FRUSTRATION

Knowing What to Sweat...and What to Let Go

As I explained in the introduction, this book is intended to help you find the tools you need to live the life you deeply desire. For me, questions are tools that can help us identify the best, happiest life available to us. I also hope to help you reap the benefits of my mistakes. By learning what to avoid, perhaps you can save time and effort along the way.

To begin, let's sort out the difference between pet peeves, annoyances, and real frustration, because the scope and the best response of these three are very different. Too often, we overreact to something that is really less problematic than we make it out to be. Too often we find ourselves responding with frustration over situations, events, or interactions that are actually pet peeves or annoyances. Too often, we find ourselves being held hostage by our expectations and, as the saying goes, sweating the small stuff. In the sections below, we'll talk about the differences between these irritants and suggest some strategies for dealing with them more effectively.

––––––

We cannot eliminate annoyances, pet peeves, and genuine frustration, but we can use them as springboards to personal development and progress.

––––––

Annoyances

Annoyances are the little things that disrupt us in a moment, but really don't play a substantial role in the grand scheme. It's annoying to get diet cola when you asked for plain cola. It's annoying when your computer is slow. Annoyances might slow you down or draw your attention for a second, but at the end of the day, they are no big deal. I look at annoyances in two distinct categories: unwelcome distractions, and things that others do that are so far removed from our paradigm, or worldview, that we simply cannot understand them.

Recognizing that these buzzing flies are not worth the focus they demand can help us keep some perspective, though it's common to get pulled away from our ideal selves by the myriad annoyances that crop up throughout the day. For me, that happens while driving. Somebody driving down the road with his left blinker on is just an annoyance, but it makes me crazy. I don't get it. I don't understand how hard it is to know that you turned the directional on. Turn it back off! To me, that's a person who just isn't being intentional with his actions. But...by taking a deep breath, I recognize that aggravating drivers are just an annoyance. They are distracting for a moment and pull my attention away from my purpose, but they don't really impact my reality. They are outside of anything that really matters in my day-to-day life. I can pass that driver and be on my merry way.

If you really look at the time and energy spent perseverating over annoyances, my guess is that you would realize a substantial portion of your week (a couple of hours at least) has been stolen from you. I know that I found that to be true of myself when I first thought of it. Recognizing annoyances and the value I was heedlessly granting them helped me to let go more quickly, and save that energy and focus for things that matter to me.

YOUR TOOLBOX:

Annoyance Strategy

The key to handling anything in your life that takes more than it gives is to separate yourself as quickly as possible. As this relates to annoyances, this can be handled with a few easy steps:

- **Take a deep breath and assess the situation:**
- **What is the cause of my agitation?**
- **How does it impact my values, my needs or my goals?**
- **Why am I giving it my energy and attention?**

If you cannot answer the "why" question, move on and don't look back. The "what" and "how" questions will help you determine whether you are dealing with an annoyance, a pet peeve, or a genuine frustration. A good friend of mine has a great phrase she uses for annoyances: "Bless it and release it." There really isn't anything else for you to do.

Pet Peeves

Annoyances and pet peeves seem similar, but they aren't. Pet peeves really get under our skin, and they hang around long after the initial stimulus departs. They call up a subconscious visceral response that most people don't even recognize. We just get agitated and uptight. This is because pet peeves challenge not just our patience, but also our personal valuation. They affect our insecurities and weaknesses because they exist right on the periphery of our personal comfort zones. For example, let's say instead of a slow computer, the problem is a buggy computer, or worse, a mystifying piece of software. Every time we try place a graphic on a slide, it bounces about the page, disappearing and half-reappearing. "How To" guides aren't helping. The instructions just aren't working. The problem seems impossible. These circumstances can make some of us completely insane with anger and self-doubt. And here's where it is important to look a little deeper. The muscle tension that creeps up our neck is not just about the momentary irritation of a dumb computer. It's about much more than that. Maybe we wish we could be the sort of person who can resolve software problems, but we're just not. No matter how hard we try to track down the source of the mysterious floating graphic, the task eludes us. Again, the world will not end if the slide set lacks awesome graphics, but this is not just a fleeting annoyance. It is a pet peeve because it is an indicator of our own personal weakness. We lack computer savvy, and that's embarrassing. No one else cares if we can flawlessly operate PowerPoint, but this kind of stumbling block is extremely vexing on a personal level.

How can you tell the difference between annoyances and pet peeves? Duration and level of vexation. Does the fuming or self-doubt hang around even after the incident has passed? That's a pet peeve. Were you able to get past the problem quickly without any lingering emotions? That's an annoyance.

A pet peeve deserves more of our attention than an annoyance. Its nagging voice calls out to be questioned and understood, because sometimes those pet peeves are really bringing to light the things we're trying to pretend aren't our flaws.

———

Pet peeves are things we're trying to hide from or deny about ourselves, usually unconsciously.

———

Like that sensitive spot on our elbows, pet peeves stick out and shriek in shock and anger when they're struck. They are in direct contact with our self-image or the way we assign value to our own character; that's why it hurts so much when something or someone smacks into it.

What we're talking about here is our personal valuation model. These are the characteristics that we think are important for the world to see in us. They make us into who we want the world to see. A personal valuation model answers the question, "Who do you think you are?" It is the sum total of what we think about our actions (and inactions) and what we hope other people perceive about those things. Qualities like intellect, competence, caring, being loved, wanted, and needed sit right at the tender core of our personal valuation model. They have power in our lives, and if we suspect they might be lacking, it's scary.

When we have weaknesses, we are either working really hard to overcome them, or we are working really hard to deny them.

Either way, when they're put up in our face, when they're called into question, they shake the bedrock of our self-esteem.

When those crucial qualities are highlighted as lacking, we're in danger of succumbing to a pet peeve. It's why we react so dramatically to something that might be small. We don't often think about how deep the emotions go. It's subconscious, deep-seated, but visceral. Thus, the response is highly emotional, largely illogical, but—at times—catastrophic to our ability to function.

To illustrate pet peeves, let's consider the mother who gets angry and then defeated when her kids whine at her. "Mooommm, I'm hungry and there's nothing to eat!" She looks over their shoulders into the cupboard and sees four different possible snacks to suggest. "I don't like those snacks," whines one child. She shakes her head and walks away in defeat, leaving him to fend for himself. That scene probably sounds familiar if you live with children, and from the outside the scenario seems fine. Encouraging kids to be independent is certainly desirable. The problem is that it creates a cycle where the children continue to aggravate the mother's pet peeve, and the mother is left feeling a sense of unresolved failure. Each repeat of the scene becomes harder for the mother to bear. Without resolution, there may be a breaking point where the mother snaps at the children, or vents her pain in a completely unrelated direction. Pet peeves, if unchecked, can build and cause real damage to the individual and others. However, it doesn't have to be a lingering irritant that continues to build internal tension. Situations like this are openings for us to learn something about ourselves and try to build new habits, if only we can seize them.

Even if you don't live with small kids, you probably recognize the sensation of clenching in the muscles or low-level disquiet in your gut. Those are signals. Your body is trying to talk to you, as mine was the day everything fell apart in my restaurant's kitchen.

Egg-gads!

Early in my career, I was head chef at a high-end Minneapolis restaurant. It was my role to supervise the cooks, ensure all food served was up to our high quality and service standards. I had a very talented cook who could work any station in the kitchen. So, that morning I put him on eggs. I had complete confidence in his abilities as a cook; however, in that moment, on that morning rush, he wasn't preparing any of the eggs correctly. Rather than dealing with the situation early in the process, I hoped it would go away. It didn't.

When we had thirty tickets up and every single one flawed, I had to send all the dishes back to start over. It was embarrassing, frustrating, and confusing. So, I yelled. I'm embarrassed to admit that in my frustration over the breakfast bottleneck, I blew up at my team. I kicked this employee off the line in a very public way. That's not how you treat professionals and I knew it, but my pet peeve had gotten the better of me.

After the mess subsided, I had to figure out what had gone wrong to cause such frustration. After some reflection, I understood that I was in a rush and didn't stop to problem solve when it would have been most efficacious. I should have recognized that we weren't working well together and addressed the glitch before it got out of hand, but I didn't want to acknowledge that there was a kink in my team that day. There's a part of me that prizes perfect performance. I want to be perceived as a capable leader, and this guy was messing up my flow! It galled me, and it prevented me from leading effectively. Upon reflection, I couldn't help but concede that the biggest part of the mess was created not by the egg cook having a bad day, but by my unwillingness to acknowledge a problem at its genesis.

Since I blew up and yelled, I had to mend the bridge I had exploded. Fear might have held me back from doing so; I could have claimed it was all the cook's fault and moved on. Many chefs will take that road. However, this approach creates resentments among the whole team. Leaving the anger festering could have meant that I lost this valuable employee and a few of his friends. Because I handled it in a very public way, I had to mitigate it in a very public way.

At the end of the shift I brought the whole crew together and I ate crow. I apologized to this person who deserved an apology. Then, I gave an earnest and honest apology to the entire team. I took ownership for my bad behavior, and I explained how we, as a team, were going to not let this happen again.

We're all going to make mistakes.

———

Any time you make a mistake, you have an opportunity to grow from it, to own that mistake and to be honest. In doing so you stand to benefit from your frustration.

———

You have the opportunity at these moments to earn the respect of your group and gain pride in yourself. Or you can shy away from it and squander frustration's potential.

YOUR TOOLBOX:

Pet Peeve Strategy

Why dig into our pet peeves if they just serve to highlight our weaknesses? To me that question is much like asking why we are advised to perform crunches when our tummies get soft. We cannot build strength without exercise, and that pertains to any form of weakness we may struggle with. Furthermore, the consequences of our unprepared and unintentional reactions can be detrimental to our relationships. Think about the last time you were really peeved. Maybe it was with your child or a coworker. How would you characterize your reaction? Were you highly combative? Angry? Lashing out? When our weaknesses, boundaries, or our personal valuation models are challenged, we can act in ways that we regret afterward. Maybe we yell at people who don't deserve it, or stomp off when the most effective solution would be calm conversation. But having our loved ones or colleagues think we are unapproachable really isn't acceptable. By recognizing that our ruffled feathers have more to do with our own personal valuation than the situation at hand, we can deal with problems more appropriately.

By having a strategy at hand, and using it to manage our responses, we can eliminate many if not all of these detrimental consequences. We can't exactly make all our pet peeves disappear, but we can decide to grant them far less power. I wasn't always this way, but over the last decade of applying this strategy myself, colleagues and friends have begun to describe me as unflappable. Restaurants are extremely high-stress environments. Rush times are incredibly busy with many different tasks to meet concurrently. Generally, I was the conductor, directing production in the kitchen, directing traffic in front of the house, and trying to make sure that everything went as smoothly as possible. It's critical that things don't get under my skin, that I don't lose my composure, that I'm not the stereotypical derisive and vulgar Chef cursing everybody out and derailing the whole operation. Someone calls in sick? Entrées incorrect? Something caught fire? I do not yell and scream. I problem solve and help everyone to move on.

All of my strategies for problem solving involve questioning myself. Just as Socrates sought to transform minds through engaged discussion, the only way we can ever become different people is to get curious about why we act as we do. The person we should be questioning is not our friend or mentor, it is our self. If we can be still long enough to quiet the chatter in our heads, we have the answers inside.

What, how, and why are three of the most powerful words in our language.

- To resolve my pet peeves I ask:
- What does this pet peeve represent within me?
- How did those self-perceptions get there?
- Why does this particular instance threaten my self-concept?

Let's apply the strategy to the above example about the mother and her whining children.

What does this pet peeve represent within the mother? Often, parents want their kids to be happy. They feel directly responsible for ensuring that happiness and providing for their child's needs. When the children are whining, it's common to make the subliminal assumption that the parent is not living up to this responsibility. While this mom might not actually think, "My child is unhappy, therefore I'm a failure," this correlation is very likely at the heart of her clenched jaw and the knot in her stomach.

How did this perception get there? Parenting is a decision and a responsibility that adults do not enter into lightly. It is not uncommon that parents will impose a whole myriad of expectations upon themselves the instant they realize that they are responsible for a life. Few endeavors will cause us to expect perfection from ourselves. It is admirable to hold yourself to high standards in anything that you do. The key to being truly successful, as well as to mitigating the consequences of pet peeves, is to be aware of the expectations you impose upon yourself, and to be honest about where they intersect with reality.

———

Expecting more of yourself than is reasonable in practice is at the heart of many pet peeves.

———

Why does this particular instance threaten the mother's self-concept? Looking from a distance, as we are doing, makes it relatively easy to recognize that the mother's need to provide and care for her children is in direct conflict with the reality that the child is most certainly not experiencing actual need. In this example, the mother can recognize that she is not failing herself or her children and begin to let go of that burden. She can also work with her children to help cultivate their own ability to get what they want through more positive means. The cool head and clarity that the mother will achieve from letting go of that which truly does not provide value will afford her the energy to improve the situation for everyone involved.

When our pet peeves are triggered, self-evaluation is called for. Ask yourself what, how, and why. The net result of this pet peeve strategy can make you unstoppable. In this example, the resolution of the pet peeve is pretty simple. Once the mom can see how the whining grates against her concepts of successful motherhood, she can look at the child and see that she really has done her job as a mom. Snacks have been provided. That, plus a few minutes of loving attention will probably solve the issue. Whining kids do not mean failed parents.

The whole point of this book is to shine a light in the dark corners, but I don't want this to come across as having to do battle with yourself. Be gentle. Be kind. Imagine taking a mirror fragment and reflecting sunlight onto your deepest fears. Don't hide from your pet peeves, because as long as we hide from them, they manifest in ugly and often painful ways.

As An Aside...
Emotional Vs. Logical Components

I think it is important to spend a little time sorting out the difference between emotional and logical components of the messages we receive. In nearly every instance, it is possible to separate incoming messages into two distinct components in varying proportions. I call these the logical and the emotional components, and believe strongly that they should be treated very differently. The logical component is all of that stuff that does not have any bearing on your self-concept or personal valuation. These are the messages received as mere pieces of data. The logical component of communication is valuable, because our personal detachment—our ability to step out of a knee-jerk reaction—allows us the ability to scrutinize the information and set it aside at will. Logical information will have more value to you as a tool because it is information that you can keep around without weighing on your self-esteem. For instance in the egg story above, when moving forward I kept an awareness of my tendency to ignore brewing problems for the sake of efficiency. Without attaching embarrassment to the memory, I tried to see that tendency as a red flag, a signal that I needed to pause and evaluate.

Emotional components are much more personal. These are the pieces that cause visceral responses and directly impact your personal sense of value and self-image. Emotional components readily become baggage, and can negatively impact our decision-making and rational processing abilities. Had I not apologized to the egg cook and my team, this memory would have become emotional baggage. When encountering a similar situation in the future, I might have felt shame at my behavior and overcompensated by yelling louder or insisting that everything was just fine, to save my ego the strain of acknowledging that I had messed up then and I would be messing up now.

The strategies in this book will be heavily geared toward making quick assessments and decisive action with regard to emotional input, while prescribing more analysis of and lingering reflection on the logical components. There is also a difference between the receipt and response with regard to these two components. With annoyances, pet peeves and frustrations, our initial response will regularly be heavily emotional, while our processing and growth will be logically driven. The goal is not so much targeted toward repressing emotion as it is about recognizing the difference between emotion and logic, in what we receive as well as how we react (memories of shame that must be dealt with versus a red flag that serves as a warning). Both components are vital, but each requires a different technique to achieve the most beneficial outcomes.

Real Frustration

When I say frustration, I am not talking about the annoyances and pet peeves above. I am talking about the kind of worry and helplessness that keeps you up at night, and makes you shake when you think about it. These are not subconscious triggering events; they are a direct response to a boundary or a blockage. This is the sort of agony that only happens when you really care about something, and are impeded from achieving it. It won't go away until you have overcome this deeply personal challenge. You need to learn to embrace these barriers, as impossible as they may seem in the heat of the moment.

————

Frustration is a signal flag showing you an opportunity to overcome. The challenge is your invitation to change, to use this obstacle to grow in character and wisdom.

————

If you find yourself regularly without frustration, odds are good that you are in a rut.

To me, real frustration is a barrier to a goal. It's something getting in the way of the path you're moving on. It cannot easily be avoided or sidestepped; it demands action. We call them roadblocks, hurdles, or the wall that you are pounding your head against. Those are frustrations, because you're trying to do something and this outside force has come in and gotten in your way. Dealing with frustration takes more personal honesty and effort than a pet peeve. It is also more blatant and external than a pet peeve. You must look hard at the cause of the frustration, its impact, and then honestly accept your role in the issue in order to achieve a resolution. Many times you will be required to go outside of yourself to overcome a frustration. While annoyances are almost completely external in nature, and pet peeves are similarly internal, frustrations will be a mix of internal and external influences. They will require focused effort, but can also yield profound rewards.

In a later chapter of my professional career, I moved beyond the restaurant industry and back to my college passion, chemical engineering. To illustrate a frustration, let me share an example from my stint as the developer of alternative fuel technology in the Netherlands. My role was Chief Operations Officer and head of technological development, so I was ultimately in charge of the process, though I relied on the expertise of a team of engineers. We were designing a reactor cell system that would make the process of burning fuel more efficient. It was highly technical, first-of-its-kind technology, and we only had a limited budget of capital and time to achieve third-party proof of concept. We had set definitive timelines to build, test and have the system functioning without any room for error. In essence, we were walking a high wire without a net.

This was familiar territory for me. I love high-pressure situations. I knew where I was headed. I had been researching this for years, and I had an excellent team working with me. We had it broken down into a series of achievable goals. The process was going well, and I wasn't going to slow down for anyone.

The first reactor cell design looked great. It was a thing of beauty. Upon completion, we immediately sent the design files to the production floor with an order for twenty-four units to complete our prototype system. I was so proud, but when we received the reactor housings and put everything inside, the cell walls were too thin. It wasn't durable for what we needed. It was a disaster. We had to scrap the design *and* all the modules that we were supposed to be testing. That failure set us back six weeks on our timeline and blew tens of thousands of dollars from our budget. It was devastating.

For the first few days, no one—especially me—could get over the shock. It took some time to regroup, to accept that we would not be hitting our original deadline. Ultimately, I had to get everyone in the room, own the fact that I pushed us to production before running a proper first article release, and apologized earnestly for the delays and added pressure that this rush to production had caused everyone. What I offered was ownership of the failure, and my personal commitment to not let it happen again. What I asked was their support and redoubled effort to overcome this obstacle.

After this, we were able to sit down and walk through the breakdown. We said, "Okay. Here's what we're seeing. What are the causes? What exactly went wrong?" We scrutinized every detail. We looked at every component, analyzed potential failure points, and kept at it until we were satisfied that we had a solution, if not multiple solutions, for each. Having that open discussion without finger pointing or blaming helped us come back together as a team.

That was how we as a team recovered, but I wasn't done yet. I was the leader of that team. I had more responsibility for the failure because I was leading the timeline and the decisions. It was easy for me to take ownership of the failure because it was ultimately my responsibility, but I still had work to do on myself.

After the team discussions, I still had to be honest with myself and ask, "What led me to make the decisions that manifested this obstacle? How could I change my decision-making process to ensure that this scenario does not repeat itself? Why did I believe that this was the best course of action?"

I had to admit, the answer was that I was simply rushing. It was the same red flag from my day with the egg cook, missed again. I'm an all-in, seize-the-day type of person, especially when it comes to business. While that can sometimes pay off, this time it really cost us. My team agreed to skip some steps in the manufacturing best-practice process with my complete blessing. We had a deadline. We had a budget. So, we didn't make *one* first article release and vet it. *We made twenty-four.* They all went in the trash.

In this example, I allowed pride and urgency to supersede established practices and better judgment. This was a prevailing tendency for me personally, which caused a great frustration and had to be dealt with. I had to admit to myself that I do rush because I trust that my research is accurate. I have a tendency to skip steps because I have been successful doing so in the past. With that new awareness in hand, I had to alter my approach with the team. I had to take responsibility for the failure, not just because I was in charge, but also because the error was mine. Because I was willing to admit that, we were able to move on and dig into all the other designs in queue. We asked, "What does this error say about the other 200-plus pieces we have designed?" We found errors there too, and this time, we corrected them before it was too late.

The final result was that I became a better engineer. I also became a better leader, because I was able to bring my team together by admitting my mistake. We were able to use the frustration as a springboard for learning and examination of our processes. Because I asked myself the extra questions:

What are the triggers that led me to skip steps?

How does this instance shine a light on my behavior?

Why would I sacrifice something this important to save a few days?

In the aftermath of the manufacturing meltdown, I was able to see the error I had been making repeatedly. I had to admit that my rush to build caused big problems. So, I slow down these days. I have tried to remember the lessons of this frustration, so I can avoid the problem in the future. These pieces of the process—understanding and honest assessment—are a big deal. This is how we grow.

The simplest way to describe the difference in strategy between annoyance, pet peeve and frustration is this:

• An annoyance is completely outside of you. Your best move is to simply move on.

• A pet peeve is processed completely internally.

• Frustrations require both internal and external action.

The old adage, *It takes a village* fits when dealing with frustrations.

By searching for the cause of the frustration and honestly acknowledging your part in this issue, you can change your behavior. Following that up with open acknowledgement and enlisting the support of others will get you beyond. Easier said than done, I know. It's scary stuff to admit your faults, but the alternative is to continue dragging them along behind you. By admitting mistakes and making amends, you can move forward freely. What's more, failure to face and overcome a frustration will guarantee that you will encounter it again!

Frustrations arise from action. They occur when you are trying and challenging yourself. They represent obstructions in our personal or environmental trajectories.

——————

That you are frustrated is a plus, because it means you are being challenged—invited to change your life.

——————

You are growing and pushing the boundaries of your status quo. In order to overcome transitions, something will have to change. You will have to change. And that can be a beautiful thing.

No one can truly attain a life worth living by shying away from frustrations.

To be clear, the topic is "Be Frustrated," not "Be Foolish." While I just made the argument for needing frustration in your life, it must be managed and balanced. Too much frustration will sap your spirits and ability to overcome. Likewise, pursuing unattainable goals is not a productive application of the frustration principle. I'm not suggesting that you pound your head against a wall. I'm suggesting that you take a step back and recognize the roadblock for the opportunity it represents. Challenges are much easier to face when we are prepared for them.

We just explored a professional example of frustration and showed how our process successfully facilitated growth. Now, I want to talk about personal relationship struggles and the methods to navigate through them that have worked for me.

In my romantic relationships, I have always been the person holding back from marriage. I worry that our culture tells a false story of love conquering all. It's as if the moment the wedding day is complete, all the problems will be over. The couple will live happily ever after: the end. I think that it's critical to a relationship, to the success, to the durability, and the investment in the relationship, to do hard work on the front end. It's not all going to be solved, but if you can't overcome the big hurdles, if you're looking at marriage as the solution to the struggles that you have on a daily basis, then my view is you're looking at it wrong.

Understanding that it's a whole lot harder to stand back and analyze a relationship frustration than a work problem, I think it's important to try to be objective. Breaking down the example above, the problem lies in the conflicting assumptions my partner and I may have about what marriage actually means. To one party, marriage might mean we fly to Europe three times a year. To the other, the same word conjures up a vision of steady employment and 2.5 children. Sussing out those differences and actually discussing them can go a long way toward avoiding major frustration down the road. At the same time, holding back from commitment causes more frustration. It's a tangle for sure, but I believe the discussion and emotional distance are necessary to see the issue for what it is without dragging along hurt feelings and fears.

I list this delicate example as another way that frustration can take deep hold in our lives and stand in the way of happiness. If we are doing the hard work of asking "how, what, why," then we can start to see the source of our problems.

———

This frustration is actually a good thing because now we're asking questions that are going to point us in the right direction.

———

The reality is, people don't get divorced because they think it's fun. People get divorced because they weren't moving in the same direction. They tried to force a square peg into a round hole until the round hole blew up. The good thing is, we can either plan to get to that goal together, and start learning how to communicate about it, or we can understand and agree that we're not going in the same direction and resolve it in a positive and beneficial way.

SECTION 2:

ADVICE

One of the greatest ways to evaluate a frustrating situation is to seek advice. It can be extremely beneficial to have an outside perspective and reality check when digging into personal development issues. This can not only provide fresh perspectives and insights, but also guard against the rabbit hole of self-doubt that such reflection can send you down. There is never any shortage of people willing to offer their advice on what you should aspire to, and how they would get there if they were you. It is much easier to find black-and-white answers when looking at a situation for which you have no personal or emotional investment and no accountability for the outcome. Advice can be beneficial; however, I urge you to proceed with an awareness of what's at play.

When receiving advice, there are two things happening. One: we're receiving logical information that may be helpful to our situation, depending on how we use it. Two: we're receiving emotional messages that can impact our own view of our self-worth. We'll spend some time dissecting logic below, but first, let's talk emotions.

The emotional component connects to all of those things that directly affect our personal valuation model and self-concept. Logical data is a tool that can be accessed when necessary, but set aside just as easily. However, emotional data is wildly irrational. It's hard to shake loose once it takes hold in our self-image, so I suggest that we be very choosy with the emotional messages we allow into our hearts.

Let's use Internet discussion as an example. If you throw an opinion out on a forum like Facebook or Twitter, you may find equally curious minds and engaging conversation. Or, you may get called ugly and stupid and be summarily shut down. Obviously, the latter can be ignored completely. Emotional input that seeks to diminish our self-concept should be allowed to have no bearing on how we feel about ourselves. However, we receive similarly hurtful, if less obvious, messages about ourselves every day. What about the loved one who disguises manipulation or guilt as advice? ("You really should eat fewer pastries. Think of your health!") Or the friend who slides insults into compliments? ("I think it's great that your family doesn't miss you when you're traveling.") How do you determine whether what you are hearing is a meaningful message, or if it simply justifies what you believe about yourself, or what the sender believes you want to hear?

Consider the source:

If advice is being offered, is the provider truly knowledgeable about the topic? Is the person generally a supportive person, or a destructive one? Is he reasonable, rational, and reliable in his overall communication?

Look at the motivations behind the message:

Are you hearing this message to be supported, enabled, or manipulated? This is critical, and not entirely easy to determine. Be diligent with asking and honestly answering this question before you grant any message value.

Measure it against experience:

You have a whole lifetime of experience, which is the basis of wisdom. Use it. Ask yourself whether the message you are receiving stands up against the scrutiny of experience.

Assess the impact over time:

Once you have determined the value that you impart to messages, you will likely make some manner of change in your self-concept, behaviors, or decision making. Don't forget to reflect on the results of those changes to see if the value you attributed to that message was appropriate in the long run. Did that advice giver continue to support and nurture your growth? Or, did he turn out to have ulterior motives in trying to change your behavior?

It's possible that within a hurtful comment, there is a nugget of truth. The family member's suggestion about healthy eating probably started out of concern for your health, but then grabbed a few personal judgments about weight along the way. I suggest that if there's even partial truth to a piece of advice, you try to rise above the hurt to see the truth within.

———

However, there is a huge divide between moving on, and rising above.

———

Moving on does not resolve anything. There is no component of letting go with moving on; nothing has been resolved, and the underlying issue still exists. This means that the next person to comment on healthy eating may trigger all of the old baggage (pain, humiliation, fear, etc.). It will come back to the surface and will compound our emotional response. Rising above any situation means facing it head on, deconstructing it and dealing with negative elements and their consequences. You have to process that pain. Yes, consider what motivations the hurtful speaker may have held and proceed with caution, but at least open yourself up to the idea that he may be speaking truth. In doing so, you think it through, process your mistake, put it into context. By processing a painful truth, you can strip the statement of any emotional power it might have over you. It pays to be aware of the impact that other people's words have on you.

Logically Using Advice

Beyond this front-line, emotional gate keeping, I believe the workhorse of receiving and using advice is logic. When we think through proffered suggestions, we can break them down in two ways:

- First, identify the key, useful element in the offering. (To continue the example above, the core message was: "Please eat nutritiously.")

- Then, re-contextualize it for yourself. ("I hate lettuce, but I could substitute apples for pastries most of the time to achieve that goal.")

Think of advice simply as a tool. Every tool has a function, and when you have a screwdriver that is not appropriate for pounding in a nail, you don't throw the screwdriver away. Rather, you find a home for it somewhere and save it for the next time you have a screw to deal with. Every piece of advice, no matter how off the wall, contains a tool that can be used for some real-life situation down the road. The bigger our toolbox, the more effectively we can handle whatever comes our way, and continue to move forward. The trick here is to identify the component(s) within someone else's litany that might be of future use. We'll come back to identifying key elements, but first I want to address re-contextualization.

Advice re-contextualization

Since childhood, I have played a little game in my head that might be helpful with re-contextualizing advice. I like to imagine that my life is a movie, and I'm one of the characters on the screen. If I'm just a player in a scene, what is actually happening right now? From an outside point of view, am I the hero or the villain? What actions led me to this point? What would the audience member eating popcorn think about the words being spoken? If I can put myself into that viewer's seat, all of a sudden the emotional impact of a situation ratchets way down. This newly removed vantage point allows me to look clearly and objectively at the warning signs and decisions that got me to this point, and to consider the consequences of my next decisions or actions.

I spoke before about considering the source of your advice. The process of evaluating a person requires first stripping off all the emotional trappings associated with that person, and asking and answering a series of honest questions. What are the motivators that help this person make decisions? What is his or her personal experience corollary to the situation at hand? Do I consider this person very successful at handling similar situations in their own life? Remember, just because the person may not have the experience or success to justify the proffering of wisdom does not make what they have to say worthless. Sometimes an ignorant perspective is just the thing to get past preconceived barriers and find the heart of a matter. Likewise, by recognizing what not to do, what should be done becomes all the more understandable.

Only when we have an accurate context of the sender, can the message be broken down. As with every process in this book, it centers around a series of questions. Only by asking questions are we ever truly able to find the answers. Here are the questions I ask myself of every bit of advice that comes my way.

YOUR TOOLBOX:

Dealing with Advice

What about their message hits home for me?

This question is geared toward separating out the emotional component from the logical. Emotional responses to advice are often subconscious indicators that a nerve has been hit. Always pay very close attention to the things that give you knee-jerk emotional responses. As suggested earlier, the emotional component should be handled differently than the logical component. Determine whether the emotional bit is constructive, or should be categorically discarded.

How can I relate this advice to the situation?

Once the emotional bits have been separated out, the remainder is data. I classify it as the logical component, but understand that not all advice will be logical, strictly speaking. We are looking at the data to seek nuggets of wisdom that we can employ as tools for current and future decision making.

How can I relate this advice to other events in my life?

This is my reminder that the tools I find are generally not disposable. By imprinting a scenario map immediately, it helps my brain trigger retrieval when similar conditions arise. Think of this as the mental equivalent of organizing a toolbox so that all of the screwdrivers share the same drawer. It makes finding the right tool an effortless process.

What sort of events can I project in which this information may be of benefit?

This is the future application of the history-centric application above. This further refines your organization and ease of access. Think of it like separating your Phillips and flat-head screwdrivers into their own separate drawers.

How will I use this information in such future events?

This question is meant to facilitate the understanding component. This is where you internalize what the information means to you, and begin to incorporate that data into your overarching paradigm.

Sometimes the true value and applicability of a piece of advice will only become clear years later when a particular set of conditions presents itself. By stripping off all the flashing and baggage, by stepping back from the heat of the exchange—but holding onto the core principle—we can lighten the load while having an arsenal at our disposal.

When I was a child, I was fascinated by this one tool my father had hanging on his wall. It was a metal band connected at both ends to different points of a handle. I never understood this tool, but knew that it had to be useful for something or my father wouldn't have had it hanging on his wall. Years later when I performed my first oil change on my own car, I was struggling to remove the filter. My father came over with the mysterious tool in his hand, and immediately it all made sense. There are bits of advice that you will receive throughout your life that will be just like that tool, which is why I place so much value on exploring every piece of logical data you receive from others.

Now, with this context in hand, let's try to get back to the idea of recognizing and retaining what is truly valuable. As your experience has already made clear, sometimes the point of real value is obvious, and sometimes it is nearly impossible to see until viewed through the lens of retrospection. Again, the process becomes easier by asking these questions constantly and relentlessly to root out the truth behind the answers. Another thing to keep in mind at this point is flexibility. What works in one situation may be exactly the wrong thing for another nearly identical situation. It is critical to amass a store of wisdom not only in the form of answers, but also of applications. Equally important is the ability to recognize subtle indicators that define any situation.

Types of Advice

There are three types of advice: unsolicited, friendly, and professional. Each generates a different emotional response that we need to be aware of before we can get to the meat of listening. People offering advice will often try to confuse this delineation, especially when giving unsolicited advice under the guise of being friendly or professional. Their perception or claims are irrelevant; all that matters is how you receive and will deal with what is given.

———

The key to listening to advice, no matter how it comes to you, is to identify what perceptual baggage your mind has wrapped it in so that you can strip it back down.

———

Once you have achieved that distance, all advice becomes the same.

It is often said that much can be learned by walking a mile in another person's shoes. In offering advice, people are giving you the chance to do just that. If you can open your mind to the opportunity, you will realize that you have very little to lose and everything to gain. Now, I will never claim that all advice is going to change your life, but you never know where that life-altering nugget of wisdom will come from. Without being open to it, you will never find out.

Unsolicited Advice

Unsolicited advice is generally the hardest to deal with. Someone walks up to you and, apropos of nothing, blurts that your idea at the meeting had some problems they want to discuss. It's hard to be graceful about something like that. Part of this is because our emotional and ego preservation responses are fully activated in the face of unsolicited advice. Your mind will be flooded with so many conflicting emotions, responses, and defenses that it will be nearly impossible to hear what is really being said, let alone listen to it. There are a few things to be aware of when someone offers unsolicited advice. Gaining true internal acceptance and control of these key concepts will go a very long way toward quieting the storm in your head, and allowing you to both listen to and hear what is being said.

First, the mind immediately develops a sensation of failure, which is often exacerbated by the fact that you are fully aware that things are not going according to plan, but were hoping nobody would notice. This is embarrassment mixed with shame. It's a tremendous emotional hurdle to overcome, and will take a great deal of effort to conquer. Failing in the presence of others puts enormous strain on your self-image, your problem-solving faculties, and your focus. The more accustomed you become to facing and overcoming failure, the better armed you will be for this circumstance.

———

This begins with understanding that failure is part of the bigger process of learning and growing.

———

However, pride is a very powerful thing, and can transform from greatest asset to Achilles' heel in the blink of an eye. It is important to be constantly aware of what your pride is telling you, versus what is really happening, and to impose reality checks as needed. Also, take a second and a deep breath to remind yourself that this response is an internal struggle. It is not associated with the person trying to offer advice. The instinctive mental and emotional response will be to focus all of this negative energy on the person for pointing out what you were trying to conceal, but that's on you. Don't kill the messenger. Acceptance is part of the process, and will allow you to move forward rather than spinning your wheels or, worse, slipping backwards. Learn to break these pieces apart, and to work through each in the appropriate way, rather than perseverating on the whole and achieving only frustration.

One other thing that makes unsolicited advice so hard to take is this: generally, the person offering advice is not the person you would turn to. There are many reasons for this; it could be a stranger, an adversary, or someone with whom you simply have not developed a strong rapport. With the proper perspective and personal reinforcement, this aspect could turn into the greatest opportunity of all. Rather than allowing your ego to overwhelm you with negative responses, try to focus on the positives. This person went out of his way to offer you the best assistance he can. In this light, intent, timing, delivery and all other tangential factors are meaningless. Focus on the reality that he did not have to do anything, but chose to. He invested the time to share some of his knowledge and experience with you.

———

No matter what his or her intent, how you receive the advice is the sole factor that will determine the outcome for you. You possess the power within yourself to decide whether it will be a positive moment for your own growth, or an opportunity squandered.

———

The mind will generally convince itself, as a matter of instinct, that there is malicious intent behind whatever advice is being given. This is not paranoia, weakness or deprecation. It is simply the defense mechanism of the ego, and oftentimes an entirely accurate assessment. This response is perfectly normal, and will occur at varying degrees any time you are given advice, especially when it hits close to home or illuminates a boneheaded error on your part. The only thing that you need to know without question is that intent is absolutely irrelevant. Take a little time to reflect on this reality, because it is one of the truths that will set you free. When you really look at it, what does it matter what the intent of the person giving advice is? The outcome is always yours to control. If you have ever graciously accepted support that was offered derisively, you know just how disarming this can be. If you have not, work at it; you will find this to be exceptionally liberating and rewarding.

The old adage that intentions are only as good as the deeds they inspire works in both directions. Good intentions can readily turn afoul if they do not manifest good deeds, and malicious intentions carry no power when they lead to works of genuine goodness.

Friendly Advice

Friendly advice comes with its own emotional trappings. Whether we like it or not, it will always be a rarity to have a friendship that can be completely honest and free of emotional meritocracy. The majority of friendships will forever be predicated on the principles of putting feelings and comfort before anything else. There is absolutely nothing wrong with this; it is merely the nature of such a relationship. Friendships are supposed to be safe havens, support in times of need, and shelter in the storm.

———

For exactly these reasons, friends are quite possibly the worst place to go for answers when you know that they will be difficult to receive.

———

A truth that is hard to hear is even more painful to give to a loved one. When seeking or offering such truths, a great deal of care and respect must be given to these burdens. Still, friends will always be the first place we turn, on the basis of comfort alone. There is still a great opportunity here.

———

Rather than turning to friends for the difficult answers, turn your attention to friends to help you form the questions.

———

The comfort provided by a close friend creates a perfect environment for turning over problems and concepts when you cannot properly articulate them on your own. Often discussions with a friend will lead down unexpected paths and open up completely new avenues of thought. I am not saying that any advice offered by a friend should be disregarded out of hand. I am only proposing that the real value of seeking the advice of a friend is not the advice, but the process. More often than not, the opportunity to seek the advice of a friend will lead to many new understandings for both of you, and prove invaluable in clarifying the issue you are dealing with.

Another value of close friendship will be in dealing with the difficult truths once you are aware of them. While it is understandably difficult for loved ones to be the bearer of a painful message, they are your best support in processing the same. In fact, sharing your burdens and trusting them to help you process this information will be empowering to them, and strengthen your bond with one another.

Professional Advice

Professional advice is the biggest mixed bag. Generally, professional advice comes to you as the result of seeking out an expert. Professional advice will come from a mentor, teacher, or some form of advisory consultant. In most cases, our desire and expectation will dictate that whatever advice you receive will be incontrovertible and given at complete face value. In seeking out professional advice, many of the emotional hindrances have already been set aside in an acceptance and realization of need. Most of the time, professional advice will be sought as a last resort. At this point, what we are really looking for is answers, not guidance. Unfortunately, learning does not work that way.

———

Learning is a process, and if you skip ahead to the answers you will certainly face the same challenges again.

———

When seeking out professional advisors, look for those individuals who answer your questions with questions, and those who have unimpeachable track records that they allow to speak for them while they turn their attention to you. Those who feel the need to impress with answers, or turn the conversation constantly toward themselves and their accomplishments, are not emotionally ready to provide the best possible guidance for your needs. There will still be value to be found in their offerings, but they will require a great deal more effort on your part.

Giving Advice

The other side of this issue, and of equal import for analysis and discussion, is the advice we find ourselves compelled to offer to others. There are two primary modes through which mentoring success is achieved.

————

The first is to be an authority on the subject matter, possessing a great enough depth of knowledge to be able to adapt the lessons to the specific needs of each pupil. True mastery also enables a mentor to adjust his or her own perception of the subject matter as it changes in the world, such that their authority remains intact through time. The second, and far more demanding, mode is to harness the unique ability to learn with the pupils.

————

In order to succeed with this approach, a teacher must possess all of the charisma, humility, and moxie of a great leader. He or she must be willing to fail under scrutiny, recover, and pass the lessons learned to the pupils, all while retaining the attention, respect and admiration of said pupils. When done properly, the attention, admiration and respect of the pupils will deepen through this process, and they will learn much more than the lesson at hand. Sadly, if more people in the world, and teachers specifically, embodied either of the sets of traits listed above, this book and all the myriads like it would be an unnecessary redundancy. We all know that bad news spreads twelve times as fast as good news, but good news (action and behavior) still does spread, it only takes a little longer. Think positive, be positive, and you will impact your environment for the better.

Rising Above

The ability to objectify situations for the sake of analysis and discovery is a skill that will get easier with diligence. I recommend starting with events that have little to no emotional impact, such as an interaction at work. Take a casual interaction with a colleague and begin to ask and answer questions about it. How did the situation occur? If I were to orchestrate the same situation purposefully, what would have been my desired outcome? Why? How close was this to what actually happened? What did I do to nudge it into the desired direction? What did I not do? (This is often the most important question!) What could I do differently the next time this type of situation occurs? What will I do between now and then to insure that I can implement what I just learned? How does all of this affect how I will face tomorrow? Take your time, be honest, and be diligent!

Any training manual worth its salt will talk ad nauseam about the five-step method for teaching new concepts: explain, illustrate, have pupil explain, have pupil illustrate, provide feedback (or some variation thereof). This holds doubly true when you are trying to teach yourself. It is very easy and enticing to cut corners, but in doing so, you are only hurting yourself. You need to recognize and be aware that everything you do influences the world around you. Any time you let yourself down or fail to achieve your full potential, you are depriving the world at large of all that you have to offer.

———

If your definition of a life worth living incorporates making the world a better place on any level, you owe it to yourself and everyone else to take your personal development very seriously.

———

I think you can see that the degree of emotion surrounding an event will drastically impact the ease and clarity with which these questions can be answered. In some situations, it may take years to reach a point where you can actually look at yourself and say, "Here is the honest answer to that question." If it takes years, that is perfectly okay. This journey is a lifelong marathon. Answering the questions is not the critical element here. Arriving at the truth is what will guide you into the future. It is so very easy to rationalize passing the buck and laying the blame at the feet of someone else, but this doesn't get you anywhere. No matter how wrong, loathsome, hurtful or diminishing the actions of another, blaming him doesn't help you clarify how you got to where you are. Blaming won't help you see what you can change about yourself to avoid such situations in the future. There are bad people in the world, there are even more people whose motivations and interests will not benefit you; accept that now and move on. You are going to encounter many people who do not have your best interests in mind, and many will take advantage of you before you are properly armed to deal with them. These are just unfortunate facts of life. Any time you spend on self-pity or blame when one does so is time wasted— nothing more, nothing less.

Let me share another story to illustrate the power of advice. After the business in Holland ended, I came back to the United States and joined a mergers and acquisitions firm. One day, a new client came to our business's table. This client was at a nexus and needed guidance, and possible financial support. My boss asked me if I had the expertise to work with these new clients. I said, "Absolutely not, but I do have a couple of resources and I know where to go to learn."

So, I buckled down and did my homework. I'm decent at research and I'm good at learning new concepts. I felt pretty confident when I contacted an expert I knew of and set up some time to ask questions. This gentleman owns multiple businesses and is highly respected for his knowledge and his wisdom. He's extremely busy and just agreeing to talk to me was a gift. Not knowing him well and out of respect, I wanted to be prepared and concise. At the agreed time, I called him and started in on my questions. After letting me speak for a moment, he interrupted. "Let me just stop you right there. I have no idea what you're trying to get from this because your questions don't make sense in the light of the industry."

"Uhhhh…" went my brain. I was 100 percent off base. I was moving in the completely wrong direction. It was extremely humiliating to waste this gentleman's time, to be so far off on the wrong path in front of an expert that I respect. To draw parallels to the lessons above, here we have an example of an emotional response to a high-pressure situation. I took a few moments to try to sort out my ego-driven feelings and put my finger on the logical steps I should be taking.

Then something happened that I didn't expect. My gracious expert reached out and plucked me from the mess I was in. He said, "Okay, what is it that you're looking to figure out? Tell me what you have learned about the business. I'll do my own research and we'll regroup in a few hours and start over." This is probably the best-case scenario for professional advice. My contact didn't have the time to pamper my feelings, but he also wasn't interested in trying to further embarrass me. He just dove right to the point, and extended an invitation to help me learn the information that I needed. In our follow-up conversation he shared with me questions that I should have been asking, and guided me towards answers I should find that would be relevant. In every instance, he embodied the mentorship of a consummate expert, and never once diminished me for my lack of knowledge. I will be forever grateful.

———

In showing me what questions to ask and where to find appropriate resources, he gave the best kind of help I could have asked for.

———

The reason I was doing the research was so that I could interview the executive team of the company in an effort to write a marketing book on their business. They were struggling to establish a succession plan for an owner who was ready to retire. They needed some help, but they felt very threatened by their precarious situation. Change is intimidating in any form, and asking for outside support is always challenging. The very first thing the president said to me when we got on the phone was "I don't understand why you're here. You clearly don't know anything about this industry." I hadn't asked a single question. "You're not going to provide any value to us in selling this business and you're wasting my time."

Here's another example of triaging emotional messages in order to be objective. I was able to put aside my own pride. I didn't react to her attack. I didn't rebut and defend myself, didn't go on the offensive with her. I acknowledged, "There's no way that I'll ever reach your level of understanding the nuances of this industry. I know a few things, but I'm really looking to you to teach me the key points, and I'm here to work. So, let's start over. Here's what I'll bring to the table. I'm here to help highlight the value proposition of your business. I can help find good advice. I can vet those people who express interest so you don't have to divert your energy away from running the business. I will advocate for you, for your future, and the prosperity of your operation—as long as you teach me what

I need to know and help me along the way when I make mistakes." In doing so, I was both giving and receiving advice in the way that she could accept it.

Now we have a great relationship, this lady and I. She actually trusts me and has remarked repeatedly that she feels so much better knowing that I'm in her court. Even though our initial steps toward advice indicated that the relationship was going to fail, now her business and her career have a future that we are all excited about.

MAKING THE DECISION TO CHANGE

Every decision is a fork in the road. You can only see so far down any given path, and once you set forth, there is no going back. Know that you may encounter resistance to this choice—even from people who love and support you. When people who love us see abrupt changes in direction, it forces their expectations to change and can even trigger their fear. This is not about you, nor is it a reflection that they don't love you or support you. Change can be hard. Even those who care for you and sincerely want the best for you will frequently speak out against your decision to change, in an effort to minimize their own personal discomfort. This noise will add strength and validation to the voices of fear within your own head.

———

If I can give you one piece of advice regarding decisions, it is this: Once you have made your decision, the best thing you can ever do for yourself and everyone around you is to forget about the other options entirely.

———

Commit your energy to making the most of the road you are on. Sometimes you will pick the wrong path, we all do. Filling your head with regrets and "what ifs" will only sap your energy, and distract you from the opportunity to learn and overcome. Other times, you will be on the right path and not even know it. If you consume yourself with the things you sacrificed or gave up to be on this path, you risk missing all that you stand to gain. Decisions are all about looking and moving forward, not looking backward. The past should be a place of peace and comfort, not a den of regret and self-deprecation.

I challenge you to consider your own decisions to change as we explore breaking the taboo in the next section.

When I made the decision to begin consulting in restaurant operations, it was a huge deviation from the life plan that I had held for years. From a very young age, I had been on a track to become a chemical engineer. As my parents so eloquently put it, "restaurant work was supposed to be a means to that end, not the destination."

What's more, it entailed a dramatic change in lifestyle: relocation on very short notice several states away, with the promise of transience for the foreseeable future. My first engagement was to involve kitchen operations realignment for a national chain. In order to accept the opportunity, I had to be willing to move within two weeks, and to relocate every four to six months. I would travel from unit to unit within the organization to bring their teams back into alignment with corporate cost and quality standards. Everyone that I knew and cared about had grown accustomed to the lifestyle that we shared, and when I announced my decision to embark on this new phase in my life, I was met with a shocking wall of resistance. Worse than that, the friends that I had been closest to were the ones most resistant to the news. Rather than sharing in my enthusiasm and supporting the exciting opportunity, they accused me of deserting them, and of being selfish. In fact, I lost some of the people I thought were my closest friends by making that decision. I was completely unprepared for the fallout of what I thought to be a relatively straightforward growth decision.

So here I was, terrified because of the major life changes that I was deciding to make. I was receiving advice from literally everyone I cared about, and a good number of people that were outside my circle of trust. Whether it was completely accurate or not, the dominant consensus that I heard was "DON'T DO IT!"

I thought long and hard about this decision, and struggled through many sleepless nights. The pressure to give up, and go back to my comfortable routine of working and hanging out with my loved ones, was immense. I was putting myself completely on the line, by starting a new business venture, by setting off to a new state where I knew literally no one, by making the decision that the status quo was not enough for me. I felt terribly alone, both as I was saying goodbye to my community of friends and as I began to settle in to my new circumstances. It was a terrible feeling, but that particular piece of the struggle was relatively short lived.

I started out with a plan, and I worked that plan. My plan included a series of short-term milestones that would help me determine whether or not I was capable of fulfilling the promise of my new career path. I set out incremental progress markers with relatively simple questions:

- *Was I able to recognize what the unit needed?*
- *Did I have a plan to overcome the challenges?*
- *Was I able to engender the trust necessary to achieve these changes?*

As I worked my plan, I was able to assess these questions against my performance. Each success led to more confidence that my decision was justified, and made the next step easier to take. After time, I began to hear different messages coming my way. I began to hear voices of support and encouragement. Some of these voices were from my friends and loved ones who were more than happy to see me succeed. Some of the messages came from within myself as my own belief in the decision grew. The most surprising messages, however, came from a new platform. Leaders, mentors, and people that I looked up to began to take me seriously, and I found myself being treated as a peer among leaders.

This was just one step in a long journey, and I knew that I would face similar struggles the next time that I chose to make a positive change in my life. I know that the only constant is change, so I was confident that that struggle would come along sooner rather than later, but I also knew that I had already succeeded once. The next time, I would be better prepared for the negative messages. I would recognize that these were not personal attacks as much as they were defensive countermeasures.

YOUR TOOLBOX:

Decision-Making Strategy

There are a few simple habits you can get yourself into to ensure that you can quash festering doubts, regrets, and distractions that could derail your new path, as soon as they arise. With time, reinforcement, and successes, you will eventually find that you don't even consider such things anymore. You will cease looking behind you for anything other than savoring cherished memories.

First and foremost, you need to do everything you can to honestly assess the decision you are about to make. As with everything, this process is most easily initiated with a simple set of questions.

How does this situation play into my long-term goals?

This question or questions of this nature will help to contextualize the decision. Sometimes when we put decisions into context we will be surprised to find that the value we originally placed on the decision is either much greater or less important than the context indicates.

How does this situation affect the short term?

This is another refinement for contextualization. This question is typically the easiest to answer, since we are in the moment, and we are predisposed to think in the present tense when decisions present themselves. This is an important question to ask, because it will get us thinking about consequences rather than the decision itself.

What are my emotional biases and how do they influence this situation?

Everything we do is tempered by our individual self-concept, and how we want to be perceived. This needs to be acknowledged, and contextualized as well.

What are the short- and long-term advantages of each option?

This question forces us to consider that there are always multiple paths to take. By considering advantages of each, it is likely that more options will become apparent. The more we consider outcomes the more comfortable we will be with the decision we arrive at, and the less likely we will be to second-guess ourselves after the fact.

What am I giving up or sacrificing for each option?

Economists have a concept called "opportunity cost" which is exactly what this question addresses. Every decision is ultimately comprised of several decisions, the decision to pursue one path and the decision to leave others behind. Both sides of a decision must be contemplated and accepted in order to move forward with conviction.

Can I live with the consequences and opportunity cost of the decision I am about to make?

When you can answer this question with a "yes," your decision has been made. Until then, you have not completed the above. Now keep in mind, the question is not "Do I love all possible outcomes?" or anything of that nature. All too often, it seems, we are faced with impossible decisions and lesser-of-evils options. Many times, being able to live with the decision is really the best that we can do. But if you cannot live with the decision, there has to be a better option; perhaps you just haven't found it yet.

The second phase of the decision-making process is what I consider the negotiation. Once you have assessed the situation to the very best of your ability, it is time to mitigate feelings of loss, maximize gains, and come to terms with yourself and the decision you are about to make. You must start by offering up concessions. You need to accept the limits of your knowledge regarding future events. You don't know how this choice will shape and be shaped by the path you are about to take, but worrying about it won't give you a crystal ball. You need to find a way to let go of the things you are choosing to sacrifice, and to retain those things you are not willing to let go of. You will need to find a way to balance your losses with potential gains, in a way that acknowledges that everything you want to come out of your decision may not be what you ultimately receive. In short, you need to find a balanced path where you can live with both the risk and the reward.

Next comes the commitment and follow-through phase. Once you make your decision, you must do it wholeheartedly. Do not allow yourself any leniency on second-guessing or backtracking. Instead, put your full focus and energy into driving toward your desired result.

Then comes follow-up, assessment and course correction. Life is a struggle. I cannot drive that point home strongly enough; you need to be mentally prepared for adversity at every turn.

———

When things are at their worst, the most powerful weapon in your arsenal is your conviction.

———

Remind yourself why you made the decision to follow this path, and realign yourself in the direction of your goals. Let your values be your compass, and your integrity your strength. Sometimes, you will stride forward with a clear head, sharp focus and all the dedication in the world, only to find that you are not moving in the direction you envisioned. That is okay, it is part of the process. Don't give in to despair or regret—this is an opportunity to learn, grow, and redirect. Consider this as another fork in the road and begin the process of assessment again. Ultimately, you will make a decision to give it a little more effort, or take a new course. The important things are to give each decision your best effort, keep looking forward, and look for lessons at every turn. When all else fails, it will be your attitude and outlook that determine where you will end up. When you are riding a bicycle and look to the left, where does your bike go? Life is the same way: If you are looking down or backwards, guess where you will be headed?

Take a moment to reflect on the decisions you have made in your life; you can begin to form a picture of which parts of this process you are already doing, and which parts you need to pay more attention to, moving forward.

Frustration's Key Takeaways

• It pays to know the difference between annoyances, pet peeves, and frustrations. Annoyances don't impact our life beyond the moments they are in front of us. Pet peeves touch something deeper within us. They literally get under our skin, which is a red flag signaling an area where personal growth is needed. With work, pet peeves can be nearly nullified. Genuine frustration, on the other hand, cannot easily be avoided or sidestepped; this type of hurdle demands action.

• We cannot eliminate annoyances, pet peeves, and genuine frustration from our lives, but we can use them as springboards to personal development and progress. Through honest self-assessment and acceptance of what we have power over, we can start to pinpoint what exactly needs to change. Usually that thing is our self.

• Advice can help put a frustration into perspective when it is just too emotionally messy for you to see with clarity. However, be cautious about which opinions you allow in. Logical information is always a welcome resource, but emotional judgments that lead with shame or guilt can negate any positive value they might have added.

Book II

Be Terrified

SECTION 1:

THE NATURE OF FEAR

There are a great many influences, factors and situations that cause a sensation of fear. It could be a life-altering decision full of unknowns, a situation that we have no control over with a risk of bodily harm, or an interaction that threatens to lay bare a mortifying weakness (whether real or perceived). Fear takes many forms, and its triggers are deeply personal in nature. What is consistent for everyone in all walks of life is that fear is the first manifestation of our subconscious recognizing a threat. Fear is an evolutionary tool, and as such is a good thing.

But, fear is also the victim of centuries of horrible PR, and I would like to take this opportunity to advocate for considering fear in a positive light. Consider, if you will, that fear is a close personal advisor, providing you with information about risks and possible threats, often before you are fully cognizant of them.

Fear is a good thing; it's what we do with this fear that ultimately defines our perception of it.

The goal of this book is to explore how to employ fear as a tool for beneficial growth and the attainment of your life goals.

To start with, let's establish a few classifications and working definitions around fear. As with frustration, we can break fear down in order to better understand it. There are fear factors (inevitable facts of life) and fear effects (our responses to that fear). We can break fear factors into three basic groups: mortal danger, threats to our ego, and threats to our paradigm. I believe that we also have four basic fear responses: fight, flight, paralysis, and denial. We cannot change our fear factors; they are the aspect of fear that needs to be recognized and understood in order to develop a positive strategy for utilizing the fear. Fear responses are fully within our control, and through proper understanding of what your fear is telling you, you can develop strategies to maximize the benefit of your fears.

————

At its simplest, fear is a signal that you need to make a choice, and that something meaningful to your person is at stake.

————

All of us are faced with choices big and small all the time. Many of us know how paralyzing it can be to worry about making the wrong decision...and so no choice is often the default option. Commercial society is full of messages and images directing us to act without worrying about consequences. We should take the leap, jump and see what happens. *No fear! Just do it!* say the commercials. Far be it from me to disagree with the astute purveyors of shoes and energy drinks, but real change—change that enables a life worth living—just isn't that simple.

When pursuing a life worth living, you're going to have to do more than ignore your fears. You are going to have to understand them, assess the consequences of your options, and choose a path. This will take work, perseverance, and the willingness to fail. I will not lie to you, even the act of facing your fears can be terrifying, but it will get easier. Success will breed success in a cascade that will make the whole process easier and less terrifying with time.

Setting aside a decision in the hopes that it will work itself out just delays the inevitable. Or worse, delay puts your fate in the hands of others who don't necessarily have your best interests at heart. This life you are living now is not a dress rehearsal; no one knows how many years they have to live. Putting off your decisions because they are scary, or because you're not sure how someone will react to the choice you make, or because it will make other circumstances harder, is no way to live.

Instead, I suggest that the work we all must do is learning to embrace our fears.

We need to look the thing that scares us clearly in the eye so we can evaluate and plan accordingly. Some fears can be discarded because they aren't serving us; others can be worked through with effort. The monumental task begins with figuring out which is which.

No one will ever be able to eliminate his fears. I don't think it is wise to try to erase or abandon our fears. Rather, we all need to acknowledge that fear exists for a reason, and it is up to us to maximize our utilization of this functionality. If your definition of a life worth living is to challenge yourself, or to accomplish an ambition, you will certainly have moments of terror. I want to encourage you to embrace the notion that hardship will happen. No, don't place yourself in unnecessarily dangerous situations, but fear is a part of learning.

I Don't Like Spiders & Snakes

The first type of fear that we characterized is mortal danger. Being afraid is natural. It's why we gasp and draw back when faced with snakes and spiders. We know that these creatures can sneak up on us and that some have the ability to kill. Fear is a protective instinct that helps us to avoid dangerous situations. For instance, let's say I'm visiting New York City, and I'm walking through bustling Times Square. Then, I turn a corner and I'm in a quiet, dark alley. All of a sudden I hear footsteps behind me and all my senses go on high alert. That is instinctive fear. This instinctive fear originates in my body's autonomic nervous system and serves as a warning signal of the potential for danger. We could find ourselves in mortal danger at any moment. This is where our fight or flight responses kick in. We will talk about fear responses in the next section, but the response to mortal danger is largely physical. Our body goes on high alert and prepares to go into survival mode. Evolutionarily speaking, that's the fuel that helped our predecessors flee from predators and learn to turn the tables and begin hunting. Some survival instincts are healthy, and should remain intact. If I were walking across a savannah, I would find myself in the grips of fear of being mauled by a hungry lion, for instance. I am perfectly content to take this fear to my grave. I feel zero need to face this fear and overcome it by strapping juicy steaks to my legs and dropping in on a pride. I would never suggest you put yourself in harm's way as a means for growth. When it comes to truly life-threatening fears, my advice is to plan to minimize your exposure.

Tangible threats

While I just finished urging caution in the face of physical peril, I think there are times when you can actually touch danger and come away a stronger person. The key, of course, is planning and preparation. That's the case with one of my favorite pastimes, skydiving. There is a whole subculture of thrill seekers who jump out of perfectly good airplanes, parachute from skyscrapers, and embark on other activities that provide the rush that comes with facing life-threatening fears.

The one thing that these people all have in common is that they prepare, train, and take every precaution to ensure that they will survive to face the next thrill. This form of facing and conquering can be exhilarating and beneficial for many. I for one absolutely love the sensation of soaring through the air at terminal velocity with nothing more than a sail of silk keeping me from a life-ending encounter with the ground below. This type of activity serves to awaken the senses, assert control, and empower a person to expand his potential. Activities like these should be regarded with the utmost care, and executed with caution and expert oversight. While I do not support or promote careless risk taking, I am a huge proponent of finding your personal boundaries and developing strategic approaches to expand them.

Tangible Fear

When the example shifts from a risk you choose to a dangerous situation you're thrust into, know that you can still come prepared. Of course, I sincerely hope that you never find yourself in a life-or-death situation, or anything resembling such. In many such cases, the wisest thing you can do is to get yourself to safety as directly as humanly possible. With that said, let's take a dive into what we can learn from tangible fear, and how we can use this knowledge to shape our desired futures.

In emergency situations like fires, car accidents, muggings/burglaries, there are the people who run away, and those who run toward danger. When you observe people who have emergency training, they are the ones running toward the danger, taking charge and managing the situation. What does their training give them that sets them apart from the average person running away from the danger? The way I see it, the difference comes from two things: core values that make helping others a necessity rather than a nicety, and possessing a strategy to focus on critical issues and make quick decisions based on their clear vision of desired outcomes.

Though I'm not an emergency responder, nor would I ever try to participate in a rescue where other, more prepared professionals were available, I believe that ordinary people like me can find greatness within themselves. In times of crisis, manmade or natural disaster, the first people to help out are usually just passersby.

―――――

Positive response to fear is not courage. Instead, courage is the outward manifestation of having a plan, and putting it into action in spite of your fears.

―――――

The strategy tips I present below are an effort to help create that capability, at least on an elementary level.

YOUR TOOLBOX:

Response to Tangible Threats

Give it a name

Have you ever noticed the power that simply giving a problem a name carries? Naming is just one of many processing tools at our disposal, but a very powerful one. Identifying a threat allows the subconscious to begin the process of establishing parameters for which data matters. This is especially important in a crisis situation where many things are happening all at once. Most people freeze when experiencing a crisis. That's understandable; when we try to take in the totality of a crisis and all of the cascading consequences, it can be overwhelming. By giving individual problems names, our subconscious faculties can begin the organizational work that they are uniquely optimized to perform. Your mind is the most powerful database manager known to man, and the process of specifically identifying a threat will set off a chain reaction of corollary processing in the background that will help you to consciously separate the wheat from the chaff. Once the tangible threats have been identified, the rest of your strategy becomes somewhat academic.

Choose your strategy and prepare for midstream adjustments

I have said frequently that the best plans are the ones that have room for midcourse adjustments as more information is received. This is especially true in the case of a crisis. It is my sincere hope that you do not find yourself in enough life-threatening situations to have it be routine. Among other things, what this means is that in a tangible threat situation, everything will be new information to you. Many of our processing capabilities are referential, so with limited points of reference, you will truly be learning throughout a crisis. Being flexible to adapting will help you to recognize opportunities as they present themselves. Having some idea of the desired outcome will keep you moving in the right direction, and will help you to determine whether an option is supportive or distracting.

Earlier in the book, we talked about the value in being specific when offering support. In this case, the paradigm is reversed, and it is crucial to provide direction in the form of very specific finite tasks. Keep in mind that the vast majority of the people around you have not prepared themselves for a crisis, and are at that very moment paralyzed by the enormity of the situation. The best thing you can do for them and everyone around is to help them give it a name, and provide something tangible for them to focus on.

Know where your boundaries are and where the exits are located

Sometimes, the best option is to simply get out of there. Even if you choose or are forced to engage, identify as many ways out as you can, and ensure that your actions do not obstruct your way out. Your boundaries will vary depending on the extremity of the threat, but will be firmly rooted in your core values. You can help yourself prepare for anything that life can throw at you by taking some time to reflect on what your core values are, and by establishing and managing personal boundaries based upon these values. This is a best practice for living deliberately, but will prove invaluable if you ever find yourself in a situation where everything is on the line. Knowing when to engage, and when to head for the door will save you a moment's hesitation, and could mean all the difference.

When the coast is clear, take time to reflect

This is so crucial. In the heat of the moment, you are largely reactionary. Once you engage, you are receiving a constant stream of new information, and responding to it as quickly as it is processed. As we will discuss momentarily, fear creates imprinted learning and most of our processing is referential. For these reasons, it is important to reflect on these extreme experiences while they are fresh. Take the time to embed important impressions of what triggers were impactful, and which responses achieved desired results. For the triggers where you responded undesirably, what options could have elicited more optimum outcomes? By processing on a trigger-point level, you are not simply preparing yourself for the unlikely event of the same trauma repeating itself; you are arming yourself with positive strategies for the much more frequent and less severe minor/intangible fear experiences.

This is an essential process, and is even more powerful if shared. Talking through the event with those who shared the experience with you can broaden everyone's experience. Furthermore, with sharing comes humanizing, and the realization that neither are you alone in dealing with the emotional aftermath, but there are positive lessons to gain from even the most dire of circumstances.

———

The fundamental premise here is that the more you understand about what you are experiencing, the better equipped you will be to quickly arrive at a strategy to deal with your circumstances, and the more deliberate you can be about guiding your outcomes.

———

EMOTIONAL FEAR, LEGGO MY EGO

Though the nervous system doesn't differentiate between potential physical threats and emotional peril, the second type of fear comes up to protect not the body, but the ego. This fear defends our ego from attacks. To make it even more difficult, the body responds the same way to an emotional situation as it would to a near miss from a bus. And our earlier fear memories can complicate matters further.

Subconscious Imprints

As human beings, we are remarkably adept examples of adaptive learning. We have sensory networks, cognition and recognition platforms that outperform the most powerful computers ever conceived. One of the earliest forms of learning that a toddler experiences is imprinting. With fear, this manifests in the form of situations like burning a finger on something hot. You only have to do it once to learn that hot objects can cause you harm, and that this harm is painful. It is sometimes fun to notice how these responses sometimes get fooled. Replace a red-hot burner with a convincing enough red light, and force people to touch it. They will fight contact, but if you can get them to touch the surface, they will invariably recoil, shake their hand in anticipation of the burn, and often cry out in pain before they realize that they have not been burnt. Our defenses are so attuned to tangible threats that the mere impression of a threat is enough to induce physical responses.

Physiological Response to Fear

As we talked about in the spiders and snakes section, our bodies have a built-in protection system that enables us to get away or fight off attackers. Under threat, our bodies may experience any of these possible conditions:

- hyperventilation
- vasodilation of central blood vessels (all lines are running full throttle)
- increased heart rate, blood glucose, serum, white blood cells, and calcium
- heightened alertness and a dampening of non-essential mental processing functions (can't focus on anything but the problem in front of us)
- piloerection (the contracting of hair follicular muscles, causing our hair to stand on end)
- constriction of peripheral blood vessels (causing blushing) supports the fight or flight responses by protecting core temperature and diverting energy to critical areas (muscles and organs), but also reflects more animalistic defenses of making us look more intimidating (consider cat and blowfish style defenses)

While in a tangible threat scenario, these physiological responses tend to be more pronounced, sometimes to the point of allowing individuals superhuman capabilities; you will notice them even in the most basic instances of fear. The drawback, of course, is that in modern society, we rarely have to run away from lions. And in dealing with aggressive humans, we may find more success using a carrot instead of a stick.

———

However, these physical responses can help us to recognize when we are feeling threatened, and provide us with earlier engagement in our fear response strategy.

———

Rather than thinking, "What's wrong with me, why am I blushing like a fool?" you can recognize, "Wait a minute, I'm feeling threatened. Where is the threat, and how can I address it?" You likely can't control the blushing, but with awareness, you can control how you respond to it.

Sometimes a threat reveals our own underlying emotional trouble spots. In these cases, it's our shame, or insecurity, or fear of loss creating a physical sensation. For instance, we're daydreaming through a green light and the car behind us honks. All of a sudden, we're blushing, angry, or sheepish. This same fear urges us to keep quiet about our ideas in meetings and often pairs with anger when we have made a public mistake. We misunderstood directions and arrive very late to an event, so that must be someone else's fault or it's traffic's fault or the universe's fault. Our spouse or partner is asking something that seems impossible, and we end up fighting rather than admitting to the fear.

What we are afraid of, in those moments, is being foolish or wrong. It feels like a lion might eat us, but we're going to survive. Having to admit our mistakes is painful, no doubt about it, especially if they have caused hurt, but running away, hiding the mistake, or avoiding this fear will not make it go away. Often, the same issue crops up over and over again, seemingly challenging us to confront it once and for all. In those repeat traumas, it's worth getting a little curious about what, exactly, is going on. Are we reacting to the situation at hand? Or is there an earlier fear memory winding itself around the problem, making it appear larger than it really is?

I want to encourage you to question yourself in those vulnerable moments. Ask not: "How can I avoid this pain?" but "How do I choose to handle the pain and embarrassment that are certain to come my way?"

When you're putting yourself out there, when you're baring your soul, when you're sharing something you believe in with the rest of the world, even when you're successful there are going to be naysayers, there are going to be detractors, there are going to be critics. Even at your most successful, you have revealed your inner thoughts and hopes to the world. There will most certainly be someone who finds flaws, someone who criticizes, someone who finds something negative to say in the best of situations. In the worst of situations, they're right.

Once you know that you are afraid, once you define that fear and you've done what you can to brace yourself for that fear or to push through it, to work past it, the next part is making a plan. Assuming that that fear comes to fruition in some way, ask, "What do I do? I'm baring my soul, I'm putting what I feel passionately about out there for the world. Someone is surely going to hate it. How do I live with that?" A big piece of what is happening in that moment is admitting to our own vulnerability. And the follow-up questions would be, "What are those vulnerabilities, and can I weather the storm of those vulnerabilities being offended?"

Remember the example from Book I about me publicly yelling at the egg station cook? Fear might have urged me not to apologize to him at all, certainly not in front of the whole staff. But I did apologize in front of everyone. I figured that a public mistake deserves a public reckoning. In doing so, I saved my relationship with that cook and with the rest of the staff who witnessed my meltdown. In fact, by embracing my fear of embarrassment, I grew as a leader and enriched the depth of the bond with my team. They respected me more because I made a mistake and acknowledged it. Had I let the situation fizzle out without saying anything, had I insinuated that the error was all the egg cook's fault, I would have missed out on that growth.

———

Change requires discomfort. We don't really grow or start to change or develop until we feel uncomfortable. You're not going to be fearless. The goal is resilience in the face of fear.

———

Sometimes we're faced with challenges and obstacles that seem overwhelming. We may not see the value of putting forth the effort to face and overcome those difficulties on the front end. When I have chosen not to face them, as I did in the kitchen that morning, I saw the immediate negative impact, not just for myself but for everybody. Once you have that "what not to do" model, it's so much easier to personally validate making the right decision. Sometimes we need that failure to surpass, that disappointment in ourselves, as a benchmark. Sometimes it's the kick in the shorts we need to do better next time.

Breaking the Taboo

A life worth living will have many terrifying moments, moments that must be dealt with rather than avoided. Just like in the case of the ego-driven fears, fears driven by what society tells us to do must be acknowledged, and in many cases can then be disregarded. Our paradigm, the underlying assumptions we hold about the world and how it works, is characterized greatly by our sociological influences, by our culture and the experiences we have as a result. Thinking critically about our "shoulds" or "can't do thats" helps us see when our behavior is guided by our own master plan, and when we do things because it's what our culture/family/loved ones expect of us. Again, it is important to recognize that there is a difference between religious and legal doctrine versus the barriers to personal growth and actualization imposed by perspective. That voice in the back of your head that says you can't do or achieve something because of who you are and where you come from; that peer pressure that forbids you from looking beyond the borders of your community; the goading of bullies and naysayers who try to pigeonhole or judge you…that's the stuff that you can challenge and overcome to great personal benefit. Challenging and changing your response to these fears will have the greatest impact, not only on yourself, but your community as you show others what can be achieved.

———

In many ways, the ability to positively break through the paradigm fear barrier is one of the defining characteristics of people who strive for and achieve true greatness in life.

———

Let me give you an example. I have recently become aware of a growing popularity of what is known by practitioners as aerial fitness, and by outsiders as pole dancing for fitness. American culture is tricky for women, especially when it comes to sexuality and body image. So much cultural pressure requires women to be beautiful, but not too sexual. Be fit so others can view their bodies and be pleased—but don't be overt about it, for heaven's sake. Women are eternally judged by their bodies first, and by their abilities as more of an afterthought.

What I have learned from the women I know and love who engage in aerial fitness is that it is tremendously empowering for them, and helps them to take control of their own self-image. I have been granted the unique opportunity (as a man) to see what is really involved, as a form of exercise. Let me be the first to say that it is a demanding total body form of exercise. The amount of core strength and muscle control required to do anything at all is extreme. There is also the personal satisfaction of taking control of their bodies and sensuality. Classes are closed to bystanders; the women not only learn a new way to exercise and care for their bodies, but they learn to feel good about themselves in a way that I haven't seen from more traditional exercise programs. I believe that a big part of the empowering effect lies in the fact that society has a prevailing conception of women and brass poles that includes demeaning acts for dollar bills and the gross objectification of women for male pleasure.

Aerial fitness, on the other hand, is all about women feeling strong, beautiful and in total control of their bodies for no one but themselves. The women I know who have broken the taboo report being more self-confident and stronger than they ever felt before. In this sense, the taboo against doing something normally considered to be out of bounds is just not necessary to abide by. I have personally witnessed the effect on individuals who have broken this taboo, and the interest and admiration expressed by others who recognize the changes and want to learn how they too can gain those attributes. Frequently the response is shock and dismissal: "I could never do that," but it gets them thinking...

———

By stepping back from the judgment of others, we can examine why we make the choices we do.

———

When a taboo is standing in the way of your best, it's likely okay to disregard it. I'm not saying it's okay to do whatever we want, whenever we want to. Some taboos exist as culturally imposed moral guideposts. Take driving under the influence of alcohol as an example. Knowing that every health authority, every law officer, and most of our loved ones wouldn't want us to drink and drive helps us remember to make sound decisions, even when we're impaired. Not every taboo should be removed, but sometimes the taboo is based on perceptions that are not complete or fully valid.

That was the case when my health necessitated leaving college. At age 20, one term away from graduation, I dropped out. Let me explain why.

My First Broken Taboo

When I was young, I was an academic. That was my talent. In high school, I learned to base my personal valuation largely on my intellect and achievements academically. I was never overly talented in sports, and did not have standout abilities in music or drama as most of my friends did. I was gifted in mathematics and sciences, so I allowed that to be the bedrock upon which I defined my value. I started college as a 17-year-old junior at the top chemical engineering school in the country, the University of Minnesota, Twin Cities, because it was the most challenging major I could think of. I was extraordinarily driven. Because of my high school work and the post-secondary enrollment option I was able to take advantage of, I was accepted into the upper-division chemical engineering program by my second semester. I was on the solar vehicle project, I was a New Student Programs Counselor, I was involved, I was active, I was achieving all of my goals.

In my third year of college, I encountered some major health issues. I missed classes due to time in the hospital, and appointments with specialists. Something was wrong with my brain, but no one could figure out what. At age 12, I'd had a cliff-diving accident injury that healed, but I had experienced constant migraines and trouble sleeping ever since. By age 19, I started suffering more extreme symptoms, including frequent loss of consciousness from the accident and the high-intensity lifestyle I had been living. I was going to school twenty-four credits a term, I was involved in many extracurricular activities, I was working two full-time jobs. I wasn't sleeping much, and I was pushing my body and my mind extremely hard. Everything just caught up to me. I ended up dropping out of school one term before graduation. My plans and my sense of personal value were crumbling at my feet.

I had to pick up the pieces; I had to try to figure out what was next, while not knowing what my long-term health would be. It was a dark time, but it was also a time for introspection. Reflecting on my health, my goals and my reasons for living, it was clear that I had to make some major changes.

––––––

I had been aiming for a prestigious science degree not because I really wanted it, but because it was what I thought I was expected to do.

––––––

Had I continued on that path, I would likely have gotten a job and kept on a steady trajectory for the subsequent fifty years. But I would very likely have hated it; at the very least, I would have lived with the nagging feeling that something was missing. Variety and challenge are what really invigorate me. I like mastering a concept, building something new, and then moving on to the next challenge. So, my body's illness became a gift to me, enabling me to stop and take stock before I spent several decades pursuing a goal I didn't really want. It could be argued that I was experiencing all three fear triggers (fear for body, ego, and taboo) at this time, with my anticipated livelihood and pride directly affected by the situation, but the prevailing fear was the catastrophic impact on my paradigm. I had built my entire value system upon a foundation of academic success, and without that, what was left?

In breaking the higher education taboo and forgoing the diploma that I had come to believe was my only ticket to success, I opened up a can of worms. My family worried for my future; so did my friends; so did I. They all expressed concern that I was making a huge error. I was truly and genuinely terrified.

––––––

One of the worst effects of this form of fear is that it plays directly into your perspective on cultural and community relationships.

––––––

A direct consequence of this form of fear is the impact and attribution you give to the opinions and judgment of others. Giving weight to other people's fears, allowing their concern to impact your personal valuation can mean that their doubt in your choices leaves you feeling like less than nothing. As I have said before, it takes a village—but what do you do when you have let your village down? In my case, I felt like a failure, I believed that I let my whole village down, and I consequently believed that I could not turn to them for support.

Breaking a taboo of this import is much different than the aerial fitness example from above. In that case, the judgment of others is trifling and completely unequal to the joy of accomplishment. And what's the risk if your hobby earns the disapproval of a few people? Not much. But here, right and wrong became far murkier. The risks were bigger and part of me believed my naysayers were correct—that I was throwing away my future. When we challenge the status quo, when we break taboos, we're going to hear about it from people we care about and trust. It's important to understand why, so we can put that concern in perspective.

––––––

The reason that you will meet resistance is that you will be forcing those around you to confront their fears and unease with change. Even those who care for you and sincerely want the best for you will frequently speak out against your

decision to change, in an effort to minimize their own personal discomfort.

———

So, I was in a real pickle. I couldn't return to school without jeopardizing my health. I couldn't walk away from school without setting off alarm bells in my head and in my community's. And then a gift arrived. So often, catastrophes like these show us that we are not alone. We have a community of people who are willing to be supportive, especially if we are willing to ask for help. In this case, I hadn't asked for a thing, but my boss showed up anyway. My job as a red-scarf line cook at one of Minneapolis's premier fine-dining restaurants paid for rent and books, but it also facilitated a friendship with the executive chef. During a shift one day, he asked me, "So what are you doing now? You've dropped out of school. What are your plans?" I said, "I have no idea."

He said, "Well, how about if you do this." Without my knowledge he had submitted a nomination for me to apprentice under a French master chef who was Le Cordon Bleu accredited, and who was only taking one more apprentice before he retired. Unbelievably, that application had won! Learning the culinary arts from a master was a tremendous opportunity, one that changed the course of my life. And none of it would have happened without a confluence of events that included being terrified, and allowing my village to help me through.

Because I have been pretty bold in my professional life, I've had many successes and even more flops. When disappointments happen, I try to look at them for lessons. They act as mile markers that I can look back on and reflect on my personal growth, check in on my goals, and correct course.

_____

The abrupt interruption of the status quo forces me to realize that often, the things that I was striving for are not the things I really need.

_____

YOUR TOOLBOX:

Strategy for Taking Risks

Unlike the reptilian terror of physical danger, I don't think you should avoid emotional peril if doing so keeps you from trying something new or learning things about yourself that you need to know, even if failure is a real possibility. It is critical that you develop a list of priorities and a strategy to face your fears.

The first step to distinguish instinctive from protective fear is to ask and honestly answer a series of questions.

"What terrifies me?"

"Is this fear based on survival or ego?"

"What can I do to face this fear without sacrificing my well-being, or that of anyone around me?"

"What fears are most directly keeping me from doing the things that matter most to me?"

The whole point here is to eliminate nonessential and limiting fears by facing them and overcoming them. Therefore, take small steps, allow yourself to fail, and pick yourself back up and try again whenever you do. I get it, people thinking ill of us is uncomfortable; failing to meet goals can bring self-doubt. Falling down is hard and messy, but acknowledging that we make mistakes is the path to self-acceptance. Sitting with our fear and attempting to understand what it's trying to say is how we change our flawed behavior in the future. Even the most embarrassing mistake, failure, or catastrophe can be used to make us better people, and maybe show something of strength and character to those around us, those we've been embarrassed by.

I cannot emphasize this enough: you will only be truly safe from experiencing fear, dread, or panic when you are dead. You cannot live your life trying to play it safe or avoiding mistakes. To do so is to live a reactionary life driven by ego rather than vision. Avoidance is not the answer. The question you ask yourself should not be, "How will I avoid pain and embarrassment?" but "What can I do to prepare responsibly so I can face my fears with confidence?"

———

I believe that fearful anticipation of mistakes is an unnecessary burden that all too often stops us before we even get started.

———

Understanding and accepting that we will experience pain and embarrassment empowers us to move ahead anyhow.

For instance, that alternative fuel technology project in the Netherlands was one that all my friends and family advised against. Engineering was my collegiate area of study, but it hadn't been my professional field for many years. And yet, I had an idea that I was certain would work. So, I made the move. I found an investor, vacated my lease, and set up shop in a country whose language I did not speak. I put everything that I had into it and got nothing out financially. Personally I achieved every goal that I set out for. I designed a system that worked. My hunch was correct, the concept proved out. It was recognized by the European Union as a whole. The company was awarded third-party validation of the new technology, the first company in the world to achieve that level of accreditation. That validation was a dream come true, but, financially, I lost my entire investment on the endeavor.

The concept worked, but in the end our partnership wasn't strong enough to sustain the bumps and bruises of the journey. Everything fell apart and our partnership was dissolved.

So there I was in a foreign country with no job and not even enough money to buy a plane ticket home. That was a terrifying moment. It felt for a while like my entire existence was in jeopardy. I was broke. I was destitute. I had to call in favors and borrow money to get back to the U.S. Coming home, tail between my legs, was deeply humiliating. I had to tell all my friends and loved ones that it didn't work out. Reckoning my own self-perception with what others were probably thinking about me was tough. They all told me I was crazy, and it seemed from the outside that they had been right.

Maybe I was a little too optimistic, but accepting the failure of the project didn't mean that I was a failure.

One thing that helped in that terribly vulnerable moment was to think of it as a chapter in my life. Sure, this chapter didn't work out the way I had planned, but it helped to remember that there would be other, future chapters.

I also had to reckon with the perception of my community. From my family and friends' perspective, I had taken a crazy risk that was destined to fail, but for me it would have been crazy not to do it, even in hindsight. It wasn't the type of project that could be done in half measures from the safety of my home base in the U.S. It was all or nothing at all. I didn't want to spend the rest of my life wondering what could have been. So for me, the risk of failure, loss of money and reputation was worth it in the end because I tried valiantly to create something where nothing existed before.

My definition of a life worth living is to make other people's lives a little better. I took the leap on that project because I believed it would make a difference in energy research. And maybe, just maybe, it would translate into real benefit for everyday users. That it didn't reach the consumer market doesn't lessen the fact that my work in the field did advance the body of knowledge in geothermal technology. I own a patent on an energy invention that will probably never be used, but perhaps the concept will further another engineer's future thinking.

Beyond that tangible realm, catastrophes have tremendous value in our personal lives because they absolutely expose our faith and resilience. Being terrified is an important part of that. I didn't go into the process saying I was going to be fearless, or that I wasn't worried about anything. A *No Fear* mantra would have been foolish. Rather, I considered all the potential worries and mitigated for as many of them as I could. It wasn't possible to make it a risk-free endeavor, but I factored in solutions for as many as I could. To me, the opportunity to try to create a brand new technology was worth carrying some level of risk.

Events like the end of my project and my financial stability could be seen as devastating. But they too are an opportunity to grow. When catastrophes happen, they show us what we have inside. A storm wipes out our house; a divorce lays us emotionally bereft; a death in the family opens up a gaping hole where there was once a loved one. Times like this are deeply difficult. Trying to move forward in an alien landscape is terrifying, and yet, these times are an opportunity to get up and try again. And they smack us right up against our values and our goals. What do we really care about? Why are we trying to do this terrifying thing?

———

At the end of the day, caring is really the essence of anything that we pursue. And caring makes us vulnerable.

———

In any relationship, caring for the other person opens us up to being cared about...or not being cared about. Starting a business is about creating a new entity, unique to an original vision, but the risk of failure always lurks. Caring is a risky business, but what's the alternative?

Passion's antithesis is apathy. If we're not caring, then we're missing a critical piece of day-to-day life. In evaluating moments like these where we have abruptly slipped off our intended track, we need to think back again to our definition of a worthwhile life. For me, I feel that successful living is providing value to my day. Providing value to my day has as much to do with the interactions that I have as the work that I do. For me to say that I have had a successful day means that I've had exchanges that are meaningful. I've achieved something that's meaningful. I've gained and I've given, and that, to me, is really the concise piece of what matters. I've never been one who cares much about objects. Nor do I care deeply about the balance of my bank account, but I do care a great deal about the value that my presence on Earth has. In a lot of ways, I want to earn that privilege.

Life is a struggle, plain and simple. We have the option to hide from this fact or face it head on and say, "I accept the challenge that life puts forth, and I will find a way to rise above whatever comes my way." If you think about it, just surviving is kind of a feat. It really is. However, if you're just surviving, somebody somewhere is providing the energy for your survival. By just surviving, by not accepting this challenge to live passionately, I believe that you're sucking value from the world around you. You're causing other people to work harder to at least mitigate the part of a struggle that you could be shouldering in their life.

Catastrophe's Upside

Pursuit of a life worth living draws on our passions—the dreams and desires we hold dear. Let's be honest: if you're not willing to be frustrated, if you're not willing to be terrified, and you're not willing to be heartbroken, it's going to be really hard to pursue your passion because action on those fronts demands vulnerability. We have to be willing to get knocked down before even attempting to pursue a dream. That's exactly what happened to me. In considering what happened with my geothermal journey, I realized that the process was, ultimately, more important than the destination. I set my sights. I had all these frustrations. At the end of the day, I didn't get where I was headed, but that journey was profound. No one else has experienced what I did. There were so many treasures along the way, both in my personal world and in the following through and doing something that I believed in, and doing something that had never been done before.

———

The surprises that pop up along the path are tangential to the main goal, but they're so intrinsic to the journey.

———

Catastrophe also shows us what support we have. Every person has a village—all we have to do is ask for help, and people show up. They may not be the people you expected to, but by reaching out, we find support we didn't think we had. My executive chef who applied to an apprenticeship for me, my friends who got me home from Europe safely, my family who have continued to love me even through my failures, all bring me tremendous comfort.

Acceptance

When I was stranded in Europe, it felt like my whole world was at risk, and to some degree, when you're in a foreign country and you can't buy a plane ticket home, it's kind of true that your whole world is in jeopardy. But **perspective** makes a really big thing seem a little bit more manageable. My world was not ending. My project was ending. Accepting that one chapter had ended and another was beginning was how I was able to shift my paradigm. It's how I got comfortable being uncomfortable with my project results.

We don't even begin to grow as people until we can accept that being uncomfortable is a part of the process. Until we are willing to be frustrated, terrified, or heartbroken, at least sometimes, nothing worthwhile will come to us. You will be amazed at how profound the acceptance of negative events will be in your overall perspective. I say acceptance, which is completely different than resignation. Resignation infers that you are powerless to the whims of fate, and takes away your responsibility to manage these negatives when they occur. You are not powerless, and although bad things will happen to you, you have all the power in the universe to make good of any of them.

Say your dream is opening your own restaurant. You've got the concept, the menu, the location, the funding all worked out in your head, but you just can't quite make the leap. What if it fails? How do you get the courage to try something that scares the bejeezus out of you?

You're going to have to invite fear into your metaphorical living room. Let it have a say in your head for a bit. It's going to tell you what? That your idea is stupid? That people will laugh at you? That you'll be losing money? That the person or idea you love doesn't love you back?

YOUR TOOLBOX:

Putting Fear Into Perspective

To gain perspective, I recommend that you write your fears down. Doing so allows you to take a step back. Distance yourself from fear and analyze the true risks here. What if people laugh? What if you aren't loved as much as you hoped? What if you go your whole life without the thing you long for? What then? Is that result really so bad, or have your goals and dreams changed as you have grown?

If the fears are indeed things you can't dismiss or let go of, are there steps you can take to mitigate the risks? Know this: you cannot avoid all risk. If you really want your goal, whatever it is, you're going to have to brave some egg on your face. Vulnerability is the only way to live the life you want because those who might (or might not) support you need to know what it is that you long for.

Hubris: A Cautionary Tale

While I am challenging you to throw off the social mores and challenge taboos, it is possible to jump into an endeavor without deeply examining your motives. On the outside, it might look like exactly what we've been talking about, but beware of hubris. It often masquerades as bravery.

Regarding your dream restaurant, society would say you're better off playing it safe. Society dictates that people should make only safe bets. "Don't bet the farm," they say. However, in the movies, heroes are those who go against the grain, especially when the odds are against them. Heck, even I like it when an entrepreneur says, "Look, people might call me foolish, but this is my dream. I'm going to do it anyway. I'm going to start this restaurant." So, what do we do with these conflicting pieces of information? Just as with jumping out of airplanes, we strategically weigh the risks and we plan carefully.

There's a smart way to go about opening a restaurant, and there's the foolish way. Having successfully run a restaurant-consulting business, I think that a lot of people fail not because they followed their dreams when they shouldn't have. They fail because they don't do the legwork. Most of my restaurant-owning clients got into the business for the prestige, but never really delved into what it takes to run a restaurant.

Part of the reason that I counsel careful risk analysis is because there's a good chance you're going to fail. You can do things to protect yourself against failure. The success stories didn't happen accidentally. There was a lot of work. There's diligence that went into that, sleepless nights. Every entrepreneurial success story talks about failures, talks about frustrations, talks about hardships and sacrifices. If you're not willing to take the risk, you're not going to benefit. I don't want you to take what we've talked about here and be foolish about it. Just like frustration, hitting your head up against the wall for no good reason is not brave, nor is it valuable. Be bold but not foolish.

Restaurants are a great example of facing fears because there are so many instances of people jumping in the wrong way. On the surface they say, "Yup, I'm escaping corporate society that was beating me down. I'm following my dream to be able to tell my friends I opened a restaurant. What's wrong with that?" Again, it's not in the cards if you're not putting forth the work. If all that money, time, and effort went for naught, that failed restaurateur gains no wisdom from being foolish. A life filled with regret isn't really a life worth living, either. There is a pitfall to misusing these challenges.

There are two tenets that I live by:
- The sum of your life is 10 percent what happens to you and 90 percent what you do about it.
- In our life, we are never given more or less than we are capable of handling.

If you can accept these two truths at your foundation, nothing in the outside world can defeat you. You are at your core the master of your own fate. Life will always be full of unexpected twists and turns, of that you can be certain. The difference comes when you decide whether you choose to perceive this road as treacherous and fraught with peril or invigorating and full of exciting opportunity.

So far, everything we have discussed has been aimed at eliminating unnecessary fears. I have told you that you can teach yourself to overcome fear through positive reinforcement, persistence and acceptance. This is no easy task, and one that can only be achieved by putting yourself in direct confrontation with your fears as frequently as possible.

Everyone seems to be aware of this in some facets of their life, but don't lose sight of how the same holds true throughout. Take public speaking, for example. Anyone who is uncomfortable with public speaking has heard the same advice over and over again. It goes something like this:

"Practice in front of a mirror. Start with small groups and work your way to larger audiences. Join a speaking or a debate group. Take every opportunity to present in front of a group, and if you can't find any, make them yourself. Prepare, practice, present, get feedback and repeat..." This is sound advice, not only for presenting, but also for overcoming all of your unwanted or unnecessary fears.

Be terrified, but be smart about it.

———

Don't expect dramatic changes overnight. Take time to recharge your batteries often. Celebrate all of the little victories.

———

Stay focused. Be deliberate in both your approach and your assessment.

If you are honest with yourself, there will always be a list of things that terrify you. It is not realistic nor is it recommended to imagine that you will, in time and with practice, learn to live without fear. Some of the things we fear are in fact foolish, and you should aspire to make these fears go away. For the rest, your goal should be to reduce the fears enough that you can allow them to become informative markers helping us to recognize that we should proceed with caution rather than forcing us to stop in our tracks.

The purpose of this book is to challenge your paradigm. I'm not a feel-good author, and this isn't a Nicholas Sparks novel. In reading this tome, I hope you'll look at yourself in a much more granular and intimate fashion, and a much more honest fashion.

———

There is nothing wrong with facing the negative, quite the opposite in fact. Facing your fears and frustrations makes you stronger and gives you a clearer view of the world.

———

Take a moment to reflect on the decisions you have made in your life. You can begin to form a picture of which parts of this process you are already doing, and which parts you need to pay more attention to, moving forward.

SECTION 3:

NEGOTIATION

I wrote this book thinking that there are really three ways of interacting with the world. First I look at me and work through what I am doing personally to be a better person (frustration). Then I start to try to bring those lessons out to interacting in society (fear). Finally, I reach toward implementing those lessons in an intimate relationship with a partner (heartbreak). Be Frustrated, Be Terrified, Be Heartbroken. That's how that name came to be.

In Book I, we discussed how to receive advice. We learned that overcoming frustration is the recipe for resilience. In this way, the work of Book I is kind of like practicing in front of a mirror. We're doing risky things, but it's mostly internal work.

Here in book number two, we're stepping out into the world. We're bringing these lessons out and trying to apply them to our interactions with other people. First, we looked at eliminating fears that just don't serve us; we cleared away the issues that don't even need to be a factor in our day, like taboo and the expectations of others. I believe the next step in overcoming fear, in being terrified, is thinking about what *does* need to be changed in our lives and what tools we can use to effect that change.

What conversations are we avoiding? Why don't we ask for raises or speak to a coworker about an impasse? Why don't we ask a spouse or partner for something we need? We don't because these conversations are scary and intimidating. And we feel scared or intimidated because we feel weak or frightened by this sense of conflict. At gut level, we sense that we might lose something from even having the conversation in the first place. So, we put off the request. We avoid the conflict. But we shouldn't. Maybe the conflict is coming from a problem that must be corrected or it will only get worse. Maybe we have a legitimate need that, if denied, will result in harm, anger, resentment, or sorrow.

Sometimes we have to have scary conversations. Negotiation is the tool we must employ if we are to rise above these potential hazards. It goes hand in hand with the resilience tools we discussed in Book I: Be Frustrated. Remember, we discussed separating emotional responses from logical ones; there is a place for both, but it's more powerful if you know why you are responding as you are. We discussed viewing your life like it's a movie, so you can get a bit of perspective on the problem that is frustrating (or scaring) you. Then, we learned about rising above a difficulty versus moving on. Rising above seeks to learn something useful from a conflict instead of ignoring the problem. Now, we are turning our bravery outward. Negotiation applies these tools that we learned in Book I, but in a broader sense.

YOUR TOOLBOX:

Negotiation Strategies

My negotiation process breaks into two halves: internal and external. Of these six steps, the first three happen in my head. The last three are the conversation with the other party.
1. Removing conflict from a difference of opinion
2. Establishing a position of strength without confrontation
3. Understand what success looks like to both sides
4. Making your needs their ideas
5. Maximizing the win on both sides
6. Closing

If I am the person initiating the negotiation, before even proposing the conversation to the other party, I am removing conflict from our differing perspectives and trying to understand what success looks like for me *and for them*. Before even proposing a conversation, I am trying to find the common ground upon which we will stand. It's less, "Here's my agenda, now get in line!" More, "Where can we come together in a way that is mutually beneficial?"

In my head, I am trying to establish a position of strength. Now, this may sound like gearing for battle, but I don't mean it to. I'm not suggesting that we should dig in our heels and refuse to be moved. But bearing in mind that these conversations are fraught with fear, I (and most people I know) have to build up my courage to even ask in the first place. By establishing a position of strength, I mean that I convince myself that it's worth having the conversation. I need to know without a shadow of a doubt that the need is real.

We hear a lot about choosing our battles wisely. We're urged to think through which fights are worth having and not having. While that's true, we should think carefully about whether our need is genuine, but rather than view it as a battle, why not an opportunity? Fighting rarely results in win-win results—whether we win, lose, or vow not to fight, that paradigm is still based on a balance of power. We've been raised to approach disagreements and differences of opinion as some kind of fight, but not everything has to be a fight. In order to be successful with this give-and-take process, we must understand what success looks like to both sides.

Think back to a discussion you had with coworkers or a group of people you were trying to accomplish something with. Was there ever a time when disagreement forced all work to stop until there was a resolution? What happened? What was the final resolution? Did everyone involved have the opportunity to make his or her case? Was there a resolution that met everyone's needs at least a little bit? I like to think that circumstances like these are an opportunity to learn something.

———

I try to approach confrontations as differences that can be resolved.

———

If you and I are coming at a problem from different levels, we're going to debate. This sort of confrontation is very intimidating. It breeds a battle rather than a win-win scenario. Someone wins and someone loses in a debate. Instead, if we think of differences of opinion as an opportunity to learn and to teach, then we can both find that common ground through dialogue. That's exciting and attractive. We think, "Yeah, I want to do that," instead of just "Ugh, this again." Just flipping that very small switch in your mind can open up whole worlds—not just for you, but for everybody you interact with.

For example, let me tell you about a situation with one of my partners in the alternative fuel business. As you probably know, environmentalists and the media are fixated on carbon dioxide and carbon monoxide emissions, and for good reasons. Our fuel cell prototype had decent results in reducing the amount of greenhouse gases produced, but those specific to CO and CO_2 were really just byproducts that we didn't have the direct control over. However, there were other exciting aspects that we did have dramatic direct impact on like oxides of nitrogen, which is much more harmful in the environment. My CEO wanted me to make promises and commitments that I didn't feel comfortable enough to make, but his job was to worry about the company's marketing and public image. He wanted to be able to report numbers that would help our public view us favorably.

I was steadfast and adamant about the fact that I couldn't give promises on CO2 because our technology didn't directly control that piece. That didn't make our technology valueless. It just meant that we had to change the script when talking to the press. We went round and round for days over this conflict. I wasn't articulating my points in a way that resonated with him. He wasn't asking questions in a way that really made sense to me. Back and forth we debated. Because we had that difference of opinion, I couldn't understand where he was coming from, and he didn't get the value in what we were doing. He just couldn't understand why I wouldn't give him what he wanted. In his mind, it wasn't a big ask. "Just give me some numbers on CO2. We do have an impact on that. What's the big deal?" Still, I refused. His resolution for this impasse was, "Okay. Well, we'll just agree to disagree."

That resolution is such a no-win scenario it really galls me when people resort to it. Everyone loses. Why even have the discussion if it's not worth the time to find a solution? I do appreciate what the CEO was trying to do—this was his way of not fighting with me. He didn't want to battle either. There wasn't any value to him in continuing these discussions because he saw conflict. He saw a fight. So, I had to try to figure out a way to remove the conflict.

First, I needed to approach the difference of opinion from a position of strength, which to me, means that my ideas have worth. By the way, so did my CEO's ideas. Remembering that both sides have legitimate reasons for doggedly holding their positions helps when we're stuck in a conflict with another person. I may be wrong; I often am, but the worth of my thoughts still exists. It's the willingness to bend but not break that holds your strength in a face-off like this.

As the scientist, I felt it was important to emphasize the most meaningful data we had. Oxides of Nitrogen (NOx) are precursors to the creation of ground-level ozone (smog) and acid rain. Ground-level ozone is a contributor to lung tissue damage, as well as exacerbating the effects of other lung diseases such as asthma. Those facts had a tremendous amount of value to me from a scientist's perspective, but I didn't realize that most people have never heard of ground-level ozone and don't know what negative effects NOx has on air quality. There's value in this knowledge, but there's no applicability. Therefore, it was correct to have strength in my knowledge, but I shouldn't have been confrontational because there was also a piece that I was missing. I needed to learn that this measurement meant nothing to our audience. It may have been vitally important to me and it certainly had value, but from a PR perspective, it meant nothing.

Part of establishing a position of strength is doing your research, doing your homework, knowing that there's justification and value behind what you're negotiating for and being able to support that. For me, much of the negotiation has happened in my head before I even begin the conversation. In researching, I'm already walking toward the center line, making concessions that are pretty easy to give up, while honing in on the essential pieces that I need to walk away happy.

Plus, it helps to remember that I have a lot to learn. I always come to a negotiation in a dialogue with strong convictions, but I'm frequently wrong. I do a lot of work upfront to know that there's a strong foundation to my reasoning...that there is some meat on the bone before I even begin the conversation. However, as in the case of PR versus science, I sometimes need the other party to educate me about what parts of their perspective I'm just not getting. Being able to say, "I need you to fill in the blanks that I'm just not getting," is a humble, yet powerful statement to make.

After realizing that my CEO and I were kind of stuck, I ultimately approached a solution from a totally new direction.

I tried to understand what success looked like for him.

I said, "Okay, look, I really understand why this is a big deal." I didn't entirely, but I could somewhat piece together why it was such a big deal to him.

Understanding and agreement aren't always the same thing.

I got why it was such a big deal to him, I just didn't agree. However, when I said, "Can we work together to figure this out? Can we do it this way?" we were able to come together.

In order to really understand what success looks like to both sides, you have to remove the assumptions. Part of our problem was that we both assumed that the other person was fighting for a solution that only had room for his idea and nothing else. I assumed that he wanted to report only CO2. He assumed that I wanted to report only oxides of nitrogen. It wasn't until we both got rid of that assumption that we were able to find a way to collaborate. For him, it didn't have to be a win of total annihilation. He wasn't unwilling to discuss oxides of nitrogen at all. He just needed information to give the press that would answer the questions they were asking. At the end of the day, that's all he wanted.

Because I was able to back up from this stalemate and see both sides of the disagreement, we were able to find common ground. His position was, "Okay, look, there's a PR side to this and we need to address that." My perspective was, "Look, there is a scientific side to this and we need to address that." I had to let go of my "I'm right" attitude and consider that there might be other ways to frame the story. I needed to hear his needs and advocate for them, too. **Because I made his needs my needs**, he stopped feeling so frustrated with me and we worked to craft a solution that **maximized the benefits for both of us**. Once we both **understood what success looked like** in this discussion, the solution was so easy, but as long as we *assumed* what success looked like for the other party, we continued butting heads. When the statement went out to the press, the message emphasized how we were providing the best of both worlds: good carbon dioxide and excellent oxides of nitrogen emissions. We gave them what they wanted first, and left them with what we wanted. My CEO and I were both happy.

Again, by approaching this negotiation as a way to come together rather than a zero-sum battle of wits, we emerged with a collaboration that made both parties stronger. In negotiation, a willingness to learn can serve as the switch we are trying to flip. In this example, my ultimate acquiescence to our public relations needs changed the conversation from "What is your problem?" to "Here's what I need." Granted, I tried to head-butt my way through this first, a common approach for many of us, but when I backed off, considered how to remove the conflict and what it might look like to collaborate, we emerged as a stronger team.

The same process can apply to our personal relationships too. A lot of times, negotiation and compromise go hand in hand, but when you can find a way to work together to strengthen both parties rather than each agreeing to give something up, the growth can be profound. Though negotiations with a loved one are typically more emotionally charged, the same principles can apply. Let's give a fictitious example that's pretty common for adult couples: disagreement over how to spend free time. Maybe one party wants to watch a football game, the other would rather go hiking than spend Sunday inside. Since football happens every week for several months, the issue comes up repeatedly. And if one party always gets their way, the other is left feeling unheard or resentful.

As with the business negotiation, the interpersonal conversation needs to begin with understanding on both sides of the living room. To truly remove the conflict from the discussion, both parties need to think through the source of the problem on their own first. Making a request for something we want can be intimidating, even with our intimates—*especially with our intimates.* So, feeling confident that we are making a worthwhile plea is important. We need to feel like our ideas have worth to feel valued in a relationship.

Therefore, we must (in our heads) establish a position of strength without confrontation.

Then, we brainstorm alternatives. We attempt to understand what success looks like to both sides. Maybe we hike first, and then revel in the rest time on the couch while enjoying the game together. Maybe we opt to split up for the day with both parties happily wishing the other well. (Grumping, "Fine, I'll do it by myself!" is not a collaboration.) It's important to note that arguments like these are not usually about football and hiking. They reveal underlying misunderstandings or dissatisfactions that haven't been resolved. So, a discussion about Sunday pastimes is very probably about a deeper issue. That's why the next steps must be taken with caution.

If both parties are engaged in an open discussion and genuinely trying to find a way to help each other out, we should start by sharing what we feel. "I really like to take these fall days to get my exercise outside." Or, "After a long week, I just want to relax and cheer for my team." *I feel... I think... My perspective is...* See how different that is from, "You never want to do what I want to do!" Because you've made the effort to understand what success looks like to your partner, it's easier to consider alternatives where everyone wins: "I'll get up early to hike," for example. The hope here is that your giving partner will reciprocate by saying, "Then, I'll make sure we get home by kick-off." When the concession is their idea, it's much more powerful because they get the added bonus of being magnanimous.

In this way, we are making our needs their idea. (It's a powerful Jedi trick to know.)

But if they don't offer, it's valid to ask for what you need. "Can we please make sure we're home by 2:00?" In this way, you're clasping them by the hand and leading them back toward the middle line where peace exists.

Usually negotiation means you're not going to get everything you were hoping for, but would you really feel good about an end result where you got everything and the other party walked away dejected or angry? In both business and personal negotiations, if the relationship is important to you, then preserving the harmonic balance will help you keep it solid. The winner-take-all approach might work one time, but no one walks away satisfied after having given everything. If it's a client or business partner, they may never ask you for anything again.

Collaboration is a signal that shows respect for the person across from you as well as self-respect. If the word compromise makes your stomach clench, that's a good thing. It's valuable to remember that respect is usually reciprocated, and to look for opportunities for mutual benefit rather than mutual sacrifice. Mutual happiness with a giving partner means that sometimes each person says, "Hey, I know this means something to you, so let's satisfy that need."

Another common pitfall in negotiations is ego. It can be a real detriment to negotiation...for both parties. To the person with the ego, that's a weak point that can easily be exploited through flattery. There have been so many negotiations in which I've gotten way more than I should have because I simply made the other person feel like he was winning. If ego is someone's driving force, that puts the power of negotiation squarely in the opposition's favor because all they really care about is that they *feel* like they won. But words of success and high stature come cheaply. Someone can pretty easily say, "How come you're so good at this?!" while simultaneously scraping all the winnings into his pocket. And for the winner, taking advantage of someone doesn't really feel good, nor does it engender a deeper relationship. Once the egotist realizes how much he lost, he'll be angry or embarrassed. And he's not likely to put energy into the transaction moving forward. For both sides, the negotiation is ruined. An ideal negotiation finishes with both parties feeling a degree of success—when the win is maximized on both sides.

The last step in negotiating is closing.

Though it's the last, it's certainly not the least step. Saying, "This issue is done" is a big deal. And everyone has to agree that it is, in fact, finished. So, when they walk away, there's nothing festering. No one is waiting for payback time. If you don't close the issue and make sure that everybody's on the same page and feels good when you all are done, then it continues to haunt you. Even if it's not brought up directly, it lingers. Unfinished business has a tendency to come back around and bite you…or precipitate something else that does.

> **As An Aside…**
> **Want to be a leader? Choose your words wisely.**
> *It's not a simple matter of semantics; the words you use affect the way you think. I was fascinated, while living in the Netherlands, by the absence of the word "if" in the Dutch vernacular. As an experiment, I decided to consciously remove the word from my own vocabulary as well, and an interesting thing happened. It started by*

replacing "if" with "when" in my speaking, but by speaking of things in such a definitive manner, my mind began to translate items from possibilities to realities in the making. Fascinated by the power of the paradigm shift that took place by simply removing "if" from my vocabulary, I began to work on other words and phrases, and found a few that delivered a profound effect to my outlook, and to my overall success as a leader. Here is a short list of word or phrase substitutions that can instantly impact your leadership presence:

Replace "if" with "when."

This seemingly innocuous shift will get you and those around you considering the event being discussed an inevitability, rather than a possibility. You will all find yourselves working with greater focus on achieving the goal.

Instead of "That's not going to work" try "How do you see that playing out?"

It is tremendously empowering to provide a safe environment for your team to make mistakes. By continuing the conversation, three things are bound to happen. First and foremost, by not shutting down the idea, you have just made it safe for that individual and everyone she or he interacts with to offer ideas, even if they don't work out. Second, you have opened the door to understand the thought process behind the suggestion, which will lead to learning opportunities for all involved. Third, every idea is an effort to solve a problem; even if the idea proves not to be viable, it gets people thinking about the problem, which will likely lead to a solution that may not have been otherwise considered.

Think twice before using "I" when discussing accomplishments and successes.

Even when you are legitimately the only one working on a task, as a leader there is always a way to share successes with your team. The greatest leaders never miss an opportunity to publicly praise and thank the people that made every success possible. This shows grace and humility, and is an act of respect that engenders sincere reciprocity. By speaking more from a "we" standpoint, you will likely find yourself thinking more about that we. This, in turn can result in more engagement with your team, producing better overall results.

Think twice before not using "I" when things go wrong.

The hardest part of being a leader is often in failing with grace and dignity. Failures, setbacks, and egregious mistakes happen even to the best of us, and a leader never forgets that accountability begins and ends with him. Avoid the temptation to call the weak link to the carpet when publicly addressing failure; that is a matter for a one-on-one coaching session. By speaking and thinking from an "I" perspective regarding accountability, you will find yourself more attuned to the details, and your team will be motivated to know that you have their backs.

Be specific when offering help.

Remember the last time someone asked if there was anything they could do? Did you reply with a specific request for assistance, or did you turn him down because stopping to think of what that person could do to support you, and explaining it to him seemed like too much effort? Worse yet, did you not consider his offer genuine? By offering to complete a specific task, you are demonstrating your sincerity and competence to perform the task, relieving the recipient of your offer of these added stresses when he is already taxed.

Start from a "yes, of course" mindset.

This was another gem I learned from my time in Holland. Whenever I made a request, it was met with this phrase. Generally, the actual fulfillment of my requests took quite a bit more effort, but I always knew we would get there. Replace thoughts that shut you off from actively engaging, along the line of "I don't have time for this" or "What now?" with this phrase. You will find yourself listening more intently, and thinking productively about the subject matter.

Make your salutations and responses personal.

Have you ever greeted someone with "What's the good word?" and received "I'm okay" or any of the myriad permutations of the same interaction: "I'm not listening to your greeting, and will provide you with a canned response that may or may not match the question"? Worse yet, when was the last time you caught yourself providing said inappropriate response? Offering tailored salutations and responses immediately sets the tone that you are present and engaged. You will notice that your own focus is more present, and others will recognize this as well.

For example, instead of "How ya doing?" Try, "Good morning, Jason. How did your project turn out?" or "How is your cold feeling?" You get the idea. Ask questions about the individual person and his life instead of generics.

Phrase it as a question.

As leaders we often fall into the mindset of needing to supply all of the answers, but when you hand your point of view to your team on a silver platter at every turn, who is growing? Lead your team to think, to question and to innovate together. Even when you believe that you know the answer, guiding your team to that answer by asking the right questions will allow everyone to think through the problem, and learn the why's behind the answer. By consistently asking questions, you open the door for everyone, including yourself, to learn.

Leaders are people moving in a direction others feel compelled to support. By constantly challenging yourself to grow, and investing the effort to move in a positive direction, you will inspire others to follow suit.

Terror's Key Takeaways

- Just like annoyances and pet peeves, a certain number of fears we regularly encounter can be examined, then discarded. Ego-based fears (like trying to save face after a mistake), or breaking the taboo (like me leaving college), are great examples of fears that don't add value to our lives. Often, they impede our attempts to build a life worth living.

- A life worth living and avoiding fear are mutually exclusive concepts. Taking risks requires trying new paths, shaking off social mores, and admitting how badly you desire something. In other words, you will have to be vulnerable. Vulnerability is the only way to live the life you want because those who might (or might not) support you need to know what it is that you long for.

- Negotiation is a learned skill, and one that will be required in a risk-taker's life. About half of a negotiation happens inside our own heads when we remove conflict from a difference of opinion, establish a position of strength from which to ask, and understand what success might look like to the other side. Then, the hard conversation happens. With practice, we can learn to make our needs into their ideas, to maximize the win for both parties, and to close skillfully so that both sides walk away satisfied.

Book III

Be Heartbroken

COMMITMENT

When talking with an advisor about this book he said, "Okay. Let me get this straight. You're going to tell me that the key to happiness is to do all the things I hate? I have to be frustrated, terrified, and heartbroken in order to live a happy life?!?" Yes, I said...with some qualifications.

I think that the key to happiness—the key to living a worthwhile life—is accepting that at different points in your life you're going to have to do all the things you hate. You're going to have to be frustrated, terrified, and even heartbroken. You're going to have to commit to the process because standing terrified at the precipice, refusing to jump, gains you nothing. You can, however, make these tough emotions less painful and less destructive by accepting that they are required and preparing for them. For instance, understanding that fear will happen when you take risks, you can know going in that it's going to be uncomfortable. So, you won't waste time and effort wringing your hands, thinking that you shouldn't be struggling. You can simply breathe through the butterflies in your stomach, acknowledge your fear without allowing it to hold any power over you, and carry on. So often, it's the way we think about our problems that causes much of our emotional struggle.

Wishing away fears and heartbreaks is a sure way to intensify them.

It is wasted effort. Knowing that, you can learn to look troubles in the eye and handle them appropriately. You can also identify growth areas and work to change the parts of yourself that don't handle challenges so well. Maybe you compare yourself to others, or get angry when something unexpected happens. Maybe you place the burden of your happiness on someone or something else. Knowing that about yourself allows you to take a pause when your specific trigger comes up. Regroup. And proceed with caution.

Yes. All of these challenges *are* hard, but they are required for happiness. Unfortunately, you can't know true joy without also experiencing sorrow, pain, and hardship. We think that by not confronting the uncomfortable issues in our lives, we're making things easier for ourselves, that we're taking the path of least resistance. Avoidance almost always turns out to be more difficult in the long run. Romantic relationships are a prime example of this kind of avoidance. We say to ourselves that we're not having the hard conversations about our problems as a way of keeping the peace, as a way not to hurt the other. We can make do with the current situation in order to make the other person happy. Sadly, if you have an unmet need, glossing over it will not make it disappear. The issue just gets worse until you can't ignore it.

Yes, hard conversations hurt. Yes, they force you to reveal your most vulnerable self, but you cannot find happiness without them. Until you and the important people in your life recognize the key ingredients to your mutual happiness and find a way to honor them, there will continue to be a gnawing feeling that something is missing. Your bright morning won't happen until you make it through the dark night. Perhaps it will be more brilliant and sweet after having been in the dark for so long.

———

I truly believe that the more you experience pain, the more open you are to appreciating joy.

———

Sometimes you just have to eat the yucky vegetables before you can have dessert. Sometimes you have to face heartbreak, because it will help you get closer to happiness.

In addition to personal growth potential, experiencing heartbreak is a superior long-term strategy against avoidance, because worry is a burden. The fear, the stress, the pressure of harboring suspicions that you could do more or be more is enormously heavy. The work of being careful to avoid the troublesome spot is never done. We say to ourselves, "Oop, better not mention that thing because it will lead to a conversation I don't want to have." "Better not think about that opportunity because I might not get it if I try..." In fact, medical research has shown a correlation between stress and inflammatory diseases like arthritis. Worry can actually trigger or worsen physical pain. However, if we take the chance and actually confront the issue we're worried about, we'll either experience joy or loss. I know that sounds obvious, but we often remain in a state of anxious stasis as a way of not having to choose. But when we do take the leap, no matter which way it goes, the worry ends and we can put down the burden.

———

So you can choose: hard work with completion, versus a burden you can never put to rest.

———

All these reasons are what I think of when I'm confronting a scary risk. Knowing that in the past, I have been better for taking the leap, I recommend that you too commit to potential heartbreak. I know, just the thought of confronting your own demons is probably pretty daunting. But there just aren't any shortcuts to true happiness.

Entitlement and Cheating

Sometimes instead of facing our trial head on, we come up with genius workarounds that might grant the illusion of fulfilling our dreams. I'm sure you can guess what I'm going to say next. Faking your way to happiness will not work because in doing so, you miss the opportunity to discover actual happiness.

Sometimes the thing you're supposed to be feeling in a moment is pain. Pain, fear, frustration are all teachers that are supposed to show you something about your life.

So, by skipping over uncomfortable sensations, you may continue pursuing a dream that just isn't right for you. For instance, perhaps a young person's family or support system always envisioned a marriage, a family and career for him, but he didn't really want that life. People who live their lives in fulfillment of someone else's vision of happiness will often find themselves with a nagging sensation that something is missing. They will likely end up creating conflict and drama, because they know that the placid struggle-free life they have been leading is not guiding them to anything meaningful. However, struggle without purpose will never lead to the growth and actualization that we are talking about here. In this way, failing to find your own dreams to pour your heart into is a form of cheating. Other forms of cutting corners and cheating are more blatant, and some more nefarious, but the personal consequence varies only by degree. We don't appreciate gifts that we haven't invested ourselves to achieve. Prizes that we haven't earned just aren't as meaningful.

Think about training for a race. For some people, it takes months and months of workouts to just get to the starting line in proper condition. But all that work and effort makes finishing so much sweeter. Knowing that you have really earned the race medal feels good, doesn't it? If you achieve something and you haven't had to overcome any obstacles or frustrations, then it's not going to have the same meaning to you. A big part of this can be directly traced to purpose and growth. The point of a race isn't to win a trophy, it is to push yourself to achieve your best. If you aren't in great shape, finishing a marathon at all is one heck of an achievement. You won't be concerned with your time compared to the athletes who finished first; your competition was within yourself, and by finishing, you achieved a great victory. By contrast, what if you decided that you were going to get to the finish line by hopping off the track in the first mile, catching a cab to the finish line, grabbing an ice cream cone, and then jumping back into the fray a half mile before the finish line? Unless you claimed first prize, you probably would not be outed. You would receive your medal, but what would it mean? This is the case with participation trophies in children's soccer. There's no connection of accomplishment to the reward of the trophy. Most of the time, younger players' games aren't even scored. So kiddos end up feeling sort of confused by the awards, or worse, entitled to them.

As adults, no one's handing out trophies, though temptations to skip steps to achieve our goals plague us. Not everyone is finishing a marathon without training for it, but they might be able to hide a few extra exemptions in their taxes, thus lowering their bill at the end of the year. Or, they might be able to have a lunch with that intriguing person without their partner knowing about it.

We tell ourselves that little allowances like that are pretty common, and who suffers from white lies? The answer, of course, is that the cheater suffers. More than that, the relationships that the cheater engages in suffer. People who rely on the cheater's integrity have been hoodwinked, and will likely lose out on their investment in that relationship, be that a matter of productivity, time, or their love.

To illustrate, let's look at a low-stakes example like weekend golf. There aren't any judges on recreational courses. Since players keep their own scorecards, cheating is pretty common. But at end of day, those false scores are meaningless. Players who end a fraudulent round at one over par don't feel what they might have expected to feel, because they know the truth. They cheated. Part of the disappointment of a dishonest scorecard is such players never know what they were capable of that day. And they lose the data that would have shown them where their game fell short. Rather than disregarding the actual data as an indictment to their public image, they could achieve these inflated scores honestly by looking at the data as an indication of where a little investment could achieve great gains. Looking at an honest scorecard could inform the individuals which segment of their game is weakest, motivating them to spend more time on the driving range or the putting green. Further, that sort of trifling deception reveals a sense of entitlement. Those weekend cheaters come to *expect* that they are amazing golfers.

The larger question they should be asking is why they feel entitled to superior scores without having worked for them.

I'm bringing up what may seem like niggling examples because it helps pick apart the way people (including me) absorb and succumb to society's expectations. We assume that we should be better than we are or have more than we have because there's a movie playing in our heads about what our lives are supposed to look like. We're Bill Murray in *Caddyshack,* murmuring to ourselves about Cinderella stories. Don't misunderstand me; there's nothing wrong with dreaming of being better. The error comes when we assume those dreams are owed to us without taking all the necessary steps to get there.

Trying to fool the outside world or ourselves with lies means that we have committed to society's vision of perfection. Trying to short-circuit the process without doing the work indicates that we believe we deserve these things. But if we haven't put in the time, or did invest time and money, but weren't willing to be honest about it...we can't expect a win. Or, perhaps it is more realistic to say that any wins we take without achieving are not durable, and the house of cards that we build out of these deceits will take very little outside pressure to topple. Going through the motions without honesty and effort *does* guarantee the pain. More than likely, it will cause greater pain to others as well.

To put a more emotional example out there, let's talk about romantic cheating. How many people have you heard lamenting that their marriage or relationship is disappointing? "I feel so alone..." "I feel taken for granted..." And so they make the case that it's better for the relationship if they go outside the union and find someone to fill the gaps. They say things like, "I'm actually saving my relationship because this other person is a relief valve." Or, "What my partner doesn't know won't hurt him/her." But of course betrayal hurts. Deeply. Few of those people had the honest but necessary conversations that might have made things better—or revealed an unsolvable issue—and yet, they still hold the expectation of a long-lasting union. These same individuals become indignant and express shock when things fall apart. They are quick to cast blame, and lament their suffering. They believe that they deserve a devoted partner to support

them through thick and thin, when they put no effort into nurturing that relationship. In contrast, had they put in the effort to share their feelings with their partner in the form of meaningful conversation—rather than the rest of the world in the form of excuses and justifications—things could have been much different. By truly investing in the relationship when the going gets tough, you give yourself, your partner, and the relationship a chance to find out what you are truly capable of. Anything less, even if it isn't as extreme as finding another person to share your intimacy with, is cheating.

———

We grow the most by exploring those tender spots in ourselves and our relationships, by risking heartbreak.

———

Papering over a problem by cheating, or lying about where we've been, circumvents the work but clings to the illusion of happily ever after. But in skipping steps, cheaters are not only robbing themselves of a chance to grow, and the opportunity for a happy partnership, they are shortchanging their partner of the same. There is no opportunity to learn with your eyes shut. Feel those heartbreaks, find out where your limits are in a relationship, and either agree to change things or decide to part ways. That's where growth happens. That's how to become a more successful person. Maybe a hard conversation does lead to the dissolution of a relationship. That can be devastating, but I would argue that it's better than living a life of conflict and guilt. Avoiding the problems in a relationship only ensures that they will repeat because the lesson hasn't been learned; the conflict can't be resolved by avoiding it. If your golf game stinks, you figure out what to practice. Head to either the driving range or the putting green. If your relationship is broken, you know what to talk about to resolve things with your partner.

―――――

How do you know when to walk away?

―――――

One might wonder, if a relationship is so hard, why keep laboring over it? In my experience, the only time when I've been spinning on a treadmill is when I was avoiding an honest answer. In my life, the only relationships that dragged on in perpetuity were the ones where we made excuses for dysfunction. In honest relationships, hard conversations happen. Each partner knows that the other will be totally honest, so forward motion or an end to the union is usually self-determining. Instead of "Whatever, honey," we say, "I know this is important to you, so I'm going to make this change." Or, "I still care a whole lot about you, but I'm moving in a different direction." In honest and loving relationships, "no" is a fair answer sometimes, because both partners know that boundaries are important to emotional health. As long as there is safety in being open with our needs, partners can express what they need, and what they are truly capable of giving. Actually, by setting boundaries and communicating them, you are again opening the doors to a happier and more fulfilling relationship for both partners. By the same token, it can help you realize that your boundaries and needs are not complementary, and that the reason for the struggles and friction you have been experiencing is that you are not truly moving in the same direction. This type of communication takes fault out of the conversation, and allows for a true sense of closure even if saying goodbye is painful.

The point is: if you don't allow yourself to be heartbroken, if you don't insist upon complete self-honesty, you won't know when the time to end things has come.

These tools all work together. If you allow yourself to be heartbroken and you're completely honest with yourself about it, the answer shows itself. That was the case in my own story.

Lost Love

I almost married once. I met this truly amazing young lady while I was in southern Minnesota, working on a restaurant start-up. She was so full of life that there was an electricity that surrounded her whenever she walked into a room. We got along famously, and from the instant that we started spending time together, we were pretty much inseparable. She used to remind me frequently to never overlook an opportunity to say "I love you" or cherish a moment of beauty. I moved back to the Twin Cities, and she had her last term of college to finish up before she could join me. The distance was a challenge, but we talked multiple times a day, and spent just about every weekend together.

When I met her, she was in the process of planning a semester studying abroad. She was planning to go to Australia, and every time she spoke of the trip and her plans she would literally beam with excitement. Over the course of our relationship, as we grew closer to one another, the prospect of this trip began to cause more worry than excitement. She worried that I would not be there when she returned, that the distance would change us. She asked me repeatedly to marry her, to tell her not to go, and to commit to be with her forever. I couldn't do it. I believed that if I held her back from taking this trip that was so important to her when we met, she would resent me forever, and that regret would tear us apart. I insisted that she go, that she experience everything that she could, and promised that I would be there for her when she came back. Upon her return, I said, we would get engaged and plan a beautiful wedding.

Sadly, the distance wasn't kind to us. Her eyes opened to a whole new world of experiences while I remained unchanged. I did not handle the distance and her needs the way that she needed me to while she was away.

The long-distance portion of our relationship happened around 2000. At that time, communication technology was nowhere near what it is today. This was years before Mark Zuckerberg forever changed the way we interact through digital media. It was the early days of cell phones; long-distance charges still existed for calls to neighboring communities, and international calling was done at pay phones using calling cards. WiFi didn't exist, and Internet cafés were just starting to emerge. When my girlfriend and I said good-bye at the end of a conversation, we did not know when we would be able to talk again. We both knew that it would take great effort on her part to be in contact, and the thought of me reaching her at all (beyond sending e-mails and waiting for her to receive them) was nearly impossible.

Things were difficult from the very beginning. I could not figure out how to be happy for her and for all the new experiences she was having while I was missing her. When I would tell her that I missed her and couldn't wait for her to get home, she felt that I resented the adventure she was having without me. When she would tell me about the amazing things she was doing, I couldn't keep up. I began to fear that I had become ordinary and diminished in her eyes. When we were together, our connection was so effortless, but communicating once a week over telephone or e-mail just wasn't the same. Messages were misinterpreted, comments that would have been jokes if shared in person took on critical implications, and we started to drift apart. Because our conversations were strained, my love found other people to share her life-changing experiences with. In the end, it was my insecurity and fear that kept me from addressing these problems when they arose. I kept telling myself that it was only a big deal if I made a big deal out of it. Because I hid my fears, my girlfriend interpreted the pauses and silences as apathy. She determined that I did not care about our relationship enough to fight for it and began the process of emotionally separating herself from me. By the time I started to fight, it was already over.

She is now a happy mother with a beautiful family of her own. She showed me so much about cherishing every single moment and living life to the fullest, and I am grateful for every second that we shared. From her I learned to never hesitate to express love and appreciation.

Most important, I learned from her that the things that truly matter are always worth the hard conversations.

When this relationship ended, accepting that it was over was a tough but necessary step for me. By accepting that raw truth, the door opened for me to recognize that I learned much from this relationship. There was joy. We helped each other figure out what we really needed in partnership. And, moving forward, I knew that while I might have struggles, I would also know joy. Struggle is a multi-iterative optimization process. That means **every time you succeed in facing and growing through a struggle, it makes the next occurrence so much easier and more developmental.**

Not all risks result in heartbreak. I have gained and experienced so much through loving. Loving, or opening yourself up to heartbreak, is founded on a principle of putting something or someone before yourself. When you give completely of yourself for the sake of someone or something that you believe in completely, you are opening yourself up to heartbreak. You are also opening yourself up to making decisions and taking risks that you normally wouldn't consider. For my part, I have lived throughout the United States, and even earned residency in the Netherlands for several years. I have experienced the privilege of mentorship, have aided in the development of people of all ages from toddlers to the elderly, and seen the world through the eyes of some truly amazing people—all of whom helped me to grow as well. I have felt so completely alive that all the magic of the universe seemed to open itself before me. I have loved completely, and I have given over my entire life to chasing my dreams. I have known the pain, the loneliness and the self-doubt of heartbreak, true. But because I accepted the risk, and gave myself freely over to the people and ideas that I believed in, I have lived a full life, and am on the path to becoming a better person.

I can say with certainty that if you also open yourself up to potential heartbreak, you will learn and grow in wild and beautiful ways. However, I understand that future wisdom is little comfort when you're right in the middle of an emotional mess. So, let's talk more about strategy for working through struggle. What does a successful approach look like?

YOUR TOOLBOX:

Stages of Struggle

Whether you recognize it or not, you have a strategy that you employ when faced with any struggle. Whether it happens in the blink of an eye, or over the course of years, our methods for processing events and the way we store and access data all come into play during a crisis. This is true for every event that our minds perceive as crisis, no matter how great or small the event is in relation to our greater reality. They guide not only our actions during a struggle but also how we will face the next challenge. People who exude calm in the face of adversity have taken control of this process. They have learned to focus their energy on efficient meaningful action, and have learned how to mitigate distractions, from outside factors as well as from their own internal monologue and emotional responses.

So what are the elements of a struggle strategy?

Pre-Engagement

Trepidation – This is where fear and emotion hold the greatest sway. There are more unknown than known variables. The weight of your personal valuation model, past experience, and assessment of necessity will determine whether you will engage or avoid the struggle. Ask: Is my unique emotional baggage affecting this situation? Have I seen this before in any form? Is confronting this issue important right now?

It is imperative to accept that this phase is where the outcome begins to take shape. It is during the trepidation phase that your "fight or flight" instincts will impose themselves upon your subconscious. In other words, know going in that you're going to be anxious, and that's okay.

Preparation – Once you determine that you are taking on a struggle, whether by choice or necessity, your mind immediately begins to prepare. Minute details come into sharper focus, and things that you didn't even realize that you were taking in are processed and categorized for potential utility. You can help this process out by taking a deep breath and relaxing your mind. Preparation can happen in an instant, or you can spend years gathering information and training yourself for a certain conflict. Either way, your best chance for success is with a clear head. Try to mitigate distractions, both internal and external, so that you can focus on the task at hand.

Engagement – Whether fully prepared or not, there is a point of no return with every struggle. Once engaged, the unknowns become known in rapid succession, and you must be nimble in the face of the shifting landscape in which you find yourself. It has been said by many a wise strategist that the best plans are fluid.

––––––

Trust in your preparation, be ready to adapt as the conflict unfolds, and focus on maximizing upsides rather than avoiding downsides.

––––––

It may seem like these are the same thing, but it all pertains to your point of reference. If you are focusing on mitigating potential problems, you will be focused on the negative, and positive options are more likely to pass you by. By contrast, if you are looking for upsides, you are guaranteed to see more options to choose from. So many of life's experiences are defined by perspective more than anything else.

Post-Engagement

Acceptance – No matter what the outcome of a struggle, the only way to move forward is to find acceptance.

Especially in the event of a painful outcome after a struggle, disappointment, emotional fatigue and the daunting journey before you can seem like too much to handle. Let me be clear, the acceptance I am talking about is not anything similar to resignation. Resignation carries with it a fatalism and finality, as though nothing can or will change the inevitable reality you have found yourself in. Sadly, resignation is one of those self-fulfilling perceptions; if you quit trying, you will most certainly quit achieving.

Acceptance, by contrast, provides an open door full of potential. Once you can accept a negative outcome, you can begin to look upon it with logic and perspective. Accepting where you are is a critical first step to plotting a course toward your destination. Now is the time for reflection on and honest assessment of what you learned and how to build upon this knowledge to achieve better outcomes in the future. Sometimes, just the knowledge that you have survived worse will help your next struggle, and other times, the lessons will be more profound. Honest reflection like this can only occur after acceptance, and only acceptance will provide you with the opportunity for better outcomes in the future.

Acceptance is a process of owning what is yours to own, and learning to move beyond what isn't.

Learning to navigate this phase of any struggle will help you to take control of your future by spending more time and energy on productive endeavors, and less energy on destructive concerns. By that, I mean that you will be focused on where to go from here rather than who you can blame for where you are.

Here, I want to insert a note of caution. In some cases our struggle is so bitter, so shocking, so unwanted that instead of finding acceptance, we dwell in a state of resentment. This stumbling block is so common and so toxic it deserves its own section to consider it carefully. Read more about resentment at the end of the Stages of Struggle, but understand that the next stages will not happen unless you can conquer these ill feelings.

Joy – With reflection comes clarity, and relief. Let me say that again: **heartbreak can lead to joy through careful reflection and clarity.** As the disappointment and emotional fatigue subside, if you have accepted and reflected upon the struggle, a strange thing happens. Sometimes it hits you like an ocean wave, and other times it comes on slowly but inevitably. Joy *will* follow the healthy processing of a struggle. It may seem inappropriate to expect or experience joy after a terrible struggle, but it is not only common, it is healthy. If you find yourself experiencing joy, it is a sign that you have not only accepted and processed the circumstance, but that you realize you are not doomed to experiencing the same fate in perpetuity. The joy is not reflective of the past, it is indicative of your realizing your future's potential.

Enthusiasm – The final phase in processing a struggle, especially one with a negative outcome, is enthusiasm. Once you know that you are better prepared to overcome adversity the next time you are faced with a challenge, you will actually look forward to the opportunity. No matter if the outcome of the struggle was negative or positive—because you learned from it, you will be eager to try your new knowledge and strategies. When you have gained wisdom, your efforts were worthwhile. Failure is an opportunity to do better next time, and even a small success will breed more of the same. Please know that enthusiasm can only be achieved after you have let go of the baggage of resentments and self-doubt. This emotion comes from an understanding that failing does not make you a failure, and that we all place a tremendous quantity more trust, respect, and value in a person who acknowledges and works to overcome a mistake than one who purports to never make a mistake in the first place.

I bet it seems odd to have joy and enthusiasm in a list of strategies for struggle, yet these key takeaways are the payoffs for opening yourself up to a process like heartbreak. Without the struggle, the relief of letting go wouldn't be so sweet. Nor would you ever want to try something similar again without having worked through the process. But if you do, you will have fresh ideas, new means of tackling problems.

You will actually want to risk your heart again.

To get to a goal, your whole heart will be required. Whether it's a new career, a relationship, or even a better golf game...whatever sparks your joy, don't be half-hearted about it. Be honest with yourself, and commitfully. The joy, the acceptance, the self-respect you long for won't come from winning the prize, but they will come because the process *is* the prize. As you work and grow, you learn to love yourself. The dream you have for your life—the one about acceptance and respect? That can only be satisfied by you.

Review & Resentment

The concept of stages of struggle creates a nice segue for a review of the ground we have covered in the text so far, and to drive home a few pertinent underlying themes in order to address one of the more challenging hurdles you will surely face with frequency throughout your life's journey: resentment. Before we dig into ideas on how to accept, process and overcome resentment, let's have a little reflection.

This book has been designed to walk you through a cumulative process of reflection, discovery, and strategy development for your future interactions. If you think about the principles of Book I: Be Frustrated, we dug into deeply personal issues. The concepts and strategies looked at the roots of our personal reactions. Continued work on the concepts and strategies of this section will help you understand and assert control over the personal factors behind how you perceive and respond to life events. In Book II: Be Terrified, we used fear triggers to explore the influence of outside forces on our psyche and subconscious decision making. By becoming conscious of these factors, and by developing strategies to gain control of your response to them, we are preparing you to live on purpose, rather than living in response to life events. Now, in Book III: Be Heartbroken, we are pushing your personal reflection and awareness into the murky depths of the intimate. This is where internal psychology and external influences hold nearly equal sway and emotion is at its peak. The concept of passion describes more than romantic involvement; rather, it encompasses that special subset of life decisions that you care about enough to place your personal interest and self-protection in the back seat. Achieving an awareness of your passion-drivers and achieving strategies to assert control over your thoughts will allow you to form deeper and more meaningful connections.

While all of these strategies, if you are true to yourself and to them, will help you to achieve a certain degree of comfort, they are not what drove me to write this book. What I have found, and I sincerely hope that you do as well, is that the culmination of this work is so much more than the sum of its parts. Once you have begun to achieve proficiency in the concepts prescribed thus far, you will learn something truly profound.

———

You will learn how to define happiness for yourself, and you will be able to articulate those very few and specific things that encapsulate what a life worth living really means for you.

———

From the moment that you know this, every decision you will ever be faced with will look entirely different. Let there be no doubt, knowing what you are truly living for will change everything about your life. Think of all the time you have spent in your life chasing things you thought would make you feel happy and fulfilled, only to be disappointed. Imagine if all of that time and energy were directed toward endeavors you knew would be fulfilling for you. This is the power you are learning to tap into.

This leads to the most difficult portion of the entire book, resentment. It is particularly challenging because in order to face and overcome resentment, one must face and overcome the darkest parts of oneself.

———

You see, resentment is as much about guilt as it is about blame.

———

There are a few ugly truths that need to be understood and fundamentally accepted: When we cannot get past the struggle with our own emotions it is because we aren't ready to accept how our own self-image has changed. We may feel guilty for having allowed the hurt to play out, for having betrayed our own sense of self, for having held a dream that just wasn't meant to be. Our teachers in life are merely holding up a mirror to our own self-deception.

You've surely heard the expression that resentment is a poison you drink yourself, hoping someone else will suffer. Again, the tired maxim is so true that it has become a cliché. But it's still true. Refusing to forgive results in a resentment that festers and steams inside of you, but has no real impact on the person who hurt you. The person you hurt the most by seething silently is you.

The sad truth is that we all do things that cause others pain. Intentionally or not, everyone hurts people that have trusted them. Even me.

As a child, I was always disturbed by the saying, "The road to hell is paved with good intentions." It seemed so counterintuitive. If the intentions are pure, how can they lead to such a terrible consequence? Then I lived the truth of the phrase again and again. I found myself with the purest of intentions hurting people that I cared about, whom I let place their faith in me. What I came to understand over time is that intentions are only as good as the deeds they produce. Where I was going wrong was not in my desire for positive outcomes, but in the decisions I made, and the things I did or did not do that led to an outcome. In digging further, I came to realize that I was hurting people, not because I wanted to, but because I took on obligations that I was not ready, willing, or able to fulfill. I had all the best intentions, I saw a need, and sincerely wanted to help; however, for any number of reasons, I didn't to do what it took to truly help.

Let's break down a few of the ways these good intentions caused hurt instead:

Poor establishment of boundaries – This is a big one in all forms of relationships, and has certainly been a biggie for me throughout life. I am a pleaser by nature, so it is really hard for me to justify standing up for my boundaries. This plays out in what I am capable of giving, as well as in what I need. By giving more than I am comfortable giving, and not asking for what I need in return, I effectively put the person I am ostensibly helping at a disadvantage. While I recognize this imbalance, and begin to formulate my own feelings of being taken advantage of, the recipient of my "help" likely isn't yet even aware of a problem. In fact, this situation establishes an unfair dynamic of "justified" resentment, without truly giving the perceived perpetrator a chance to meet your needs.

Inadequate understanding of the need – Sometimes, our resentment is the product of feeling unappreciated. When this is the case, it is very likely that the help being provided isn't the help that is needed. When you give of yourself in a genuine attempt to help, and your efforts are not appreciated, it hurts. We feel devalued or discredited, and this hurts. Frequently, the recipient of your help either was not receiving the help that they needed, or was not emotionally prepared to receive the help that they needed. When you find yourself harboring resentment for these reasons, it is likely that your motivations were rooted in what you expected to receive, rather than what you were willing to give.

Failure to align expectations – If the involved parties do not clearly articulate and agree upon expectations at the onset of an engagement, at least one involved party will end up feeling taken advantage of. Every interaction, either business or personal, in which I have failed to have clear and open discussions about expectations, has resulted in some level of consternation.

Recipient does not want help – Have you ever told someone exactly what he needed to hear, and been resented for it? It is essential that you are sensitive to the needs and emotional status of someone before you try to offer your definition of help. If you aren't comfortable having a discussion with him about his journey and the place he currently finds himself, there is a good chance that you are not in a safe enough relationship to force a breakthrough conversation.

Letting go of resentment is more about forgiving yourself than forgiving the person you blame.

Resentment is the manifestation of a victim paradigm. It is ultimately rooted in your giving away power and control of your happiness, your present status, and ultimately your sense of value to whatever or whoever you are feeling resentment toward. Now, before you get defensive or self-effacing, please understand that we all do this. We are all hurt and disappointed by people and life events from time to time. This pain is real, and it is completely normal to feel resentment for the things that cause us pain. It is also all too common that some people will not even have good intentions when they hurt you. You cannot stop yourself from being hurt. What you can do is learn to control what you do once you have been hurt. Every ounce of energy and power you give to carrying resentment, and blaming others for your pain, is energy that you are not spending learning, recovering, and healing. Rather than perseverating on self-defeating and toxic lines of thought, try exploring yourself.

Some questions worth considering:

- **What was I expecting, and did I do everything I could to achieve it?**
- **What conversations did I not have on the way to where I am now?**
- **What were some early warnings that this was going down the wrong path?**
- **What can I do differently to realign our course?**

Keep in mind that the purpose of these questions is to learn and grow, not to beat yourself up, or justify self-pity. You will reap what you sow, and if you commit to overcoming, you will.

SECTION 2:

FINDING YOUR INNATE VALUE AMIDST FAILURE

Truly having your heart broken is one of the hardest experiences in life. It physically aches; in fact, functional MRI scans of people who were broken up with show higher than normal activity in the pain-sensing areas of the brain. The same neurochemicals that make falling in love deliriously delicious, when abruptly interrupted leave us in dopamine withdrawal, desperate for the lost love who can make us feel whole again. Heartbreak, whether romantic or professional, is *not* just in your head.

Surviving such an ordeal reveals your character. It shows you the deepest level of who you are. It peels away all your energy for trifling pursuits; heartbreak boils your life down to the things that really matter.

Thus, heartbreak reaffirms the strength of your village.

When you're bare and raw like this, everything comes into crisp focus. You recognize the value of the life that you've cultivated and the people in your network who continue to support you. You recognize your ability to overcome. You recognize that you have to honestly face your flaws. People often celebrate the characteristics that surface in the face of success, like honesty, clarity and self-awareness. "I was right!" we say. But the flip side is just as true. Clarity, honesty, and self-awareness can be tricky to pin down when you fail. When we are feeling miserable, the last thing we want to be reminded of is our own complicity in getting there. We want someone to blame; we want someone to tell us that it isn't our fault. We want an easy end to the pain, but this is no place for half measures. Truly giving everything you have to something and failing at it is tremendously valuable once you can say to yourself, "This approach does not work. I don't ever have to try that again, because now I know." Definitive answers are rare. Take heart in the knowledge you have gained.

I have people tell me all the time that I shouldn't use words like "failure" because they are too derogatory. I challenge every one of them to find me one successful or happy person who hasn't grown comfortable with the concept that she is fallible. To take it one step further, try to come up with a single success story that does not begin in failure. There is no logical argument I can think of to support the notion that openly admitting to failure is more diminishing than the abject denial of failure in any form. I would argue that there is a great deal of evidence that the opposite is true. Again, it is not so much a matter of recognizing that you failed in an endeavor, it is all about being able to separate yourself from the failure, learning from it, and preparing for the next challenge.

One of the positive things about truly being heartbroken is that it forces you to step back and take stock. When you truly look at your life, you find that though it feels like everything fell apart there is still much to be grateful for. You can say, "I still have this. I still am this. I still know this. I've gained this." That inventory can act as a balm to your broken heart. You may have started out wallowing and feeling bad, but you can end with a prayer of humility and gratitude. It's so easy to say, "Clearly I'm worthless because this person doesn't love me anymore," or, "Clearly I'm a failure because I put every ounce of myself into this and it failed, which means that I am a failure." That's one way to look at it, but it's not the only way. More than that, it's not a healthy or productive way. If you can turn off the pressures that come from outside voices—from society's expectations—you can look for the facts of a situation. But that's not always easy.

The ego doesn't just drive you to think that you're special.

The ego also drives you to think that you're worthless.

The ego is the thing that leads people to despair. They think, "My love broke up with me. Clearly, I'm not worth a damn, and I'll never be loved again." Statements like that indicate that the ego is in the driver's seat. When/if you can remove ego, you can say to yourself, "I'm not going to let my thoughts drive me crazy. I'm not going to let my ego drive my actions. I'm going to look at it from a more distant point of view." Say, "Wait a minute. What am I left with here? I'm still me. I still feel good about my effort. I put myself on the line. At least I risked myself trying to succeed. That I failed doesn't take away my bravery. At least I was willing to follow my passion even if I did leave myself heartbroken. I can be better for that."

Introducing Logic into an Emotional Storm

In Book I, we talked about emotional versus logical components with regard to frustration. Knowing the difference becomes even more vital when dealing with heartbreak. There's a certain point at which we have to accept that some bad things are true. Each one of us is human, full of flaws and attributes we wish were different. And each one of us engages with other fallible humans with their grab bags filled with fatal flaws. However, those facts don't have to function as anchors that weigh our future down. We can look for the positive elements. In choosing to see the hardest aspects of life in a positive way, we're not refusing to see the truth. We're reframing events as lessons so we can actually use them to grow instead of beating ourselves up with them. Say a woman lied to her husband and got caught. She could say, "I'm a terrible person and I don't deserve the life I have." Or, "I made a terrible choice, but next time I will be honest, even if it's hard." We reframe so we can move forward and grow from our mistakes.

Having said that, let me urge caution. Failure is one of those places where logic can be your biggest enemy. I fall victim to this more often than I'd like. For instance, when I moved to the Netherlands, my entire support network told me it was a bad idea. When their predictions came true, part of me figured that they were right, that I was wrong to try for my dream. I figured it must have been my ego that sent me on a wild goose chase. Round and round I went in my head; I drove myself crazy for a while. I equated the concern my loved ones had for me in taking a huge risk with doubt in my capabilities, and in the viability of my idea. I then viewed my failure as a validation of those perceived doubts. From here, I had already stepped off the cliff, and was fast spiraling into the "logical" conclusion that I failed because I was a failure who had clearly overestimated my own value. It's really easy to create logical arguments for negative outcomes. In that way, logic can be an enemy in failure. But we must take care not to use our own stories as weapons.

It's easy to justify giving up based on what seems like logic. One of the internal conversations I had then sounded like, "You know what? I should just give up. I'm going to take an easy road from now on because clearly I am mediocre." In my personal paradigm, being mediocre is probably the worst insult I could ever receive. Though the thoughts are unkind, when my logic is fueled by shame that's what happens. Over time, I have recognized this pattern in my thinking. Once noticed, I try not to hang out there in "Why Bother Land."

———

Because the thing is, no matter how successful I am in my endeavors, there will always be some person for whom my accomplishments are not good enough.

———

Someone will always be ready to tell me that I stink and I shouldn't even bother trying. If I'm looking for confirmation of my doubts, I will always find someone glad to oblige.

The irony of all of this self-deprecation is that it completely negates not only all of the amazing things that you actually do achieve, but also all of the people who love, trust and believe in you. For my part, by considering the project an abject failure, I had to disregard that my team and I were the first people in the history of the world to achieve third-party validation for a new combustion technology. That is just silly, but worse than that, by claiming foolishness for even trying, I was essentially telling everyone on my team, my investors, and everyone who believed in and supported the effort, that they were fools. Clearly, this was not the case. I worked with some amazing minds and extraordinary people on this project. The only way to praise their achievement was to accept a little myself. Failure is seldom complete, and as I preach accepting failure, I feel equally strongly that you must accurately define what failed. This is a big part of finding the lessons.

When the cycle of self-accusation starts to happen in my head, I recognize it for the emotional bad habit that it is. That's when it can be helpful to pull out paper and pen and actually make lists. What happened? Gains and losses of a failed job? Pluses and minuses of being dumped... Whatever it is, it's important to write it down because in my head, emotional weight is attached to every item.

"I lost *x*" on paper is just that, a math calculation. Inside "I'm No Good Land," the phrase *I failed* is attached to so many fears. It's an accusation about what others have said about me, it's a reminder of the time I bounced a check, and that time in middle school football when I dropped a punt...and...and... That road ends at "I'm just no good!" That's why paper is better for these exercises. It gets scary inside our heads.

———

We are conditioned from infancy to find what's wrong. That is habit for each of us, but identifying what's right and good is truly a challenge.

———

Writing down a tally sheet forces us to look for the good, it re-conditions our thinking, and opens the door for constructive dialogue, both within yourself and with others.

You may think the crazy-brain-train is hyperbolic because you don't consciously think about every event related to failing when you make a mistake, or the subconscious implications on your self-valuation. I'm sure that's true, you probably don't think it all out consciously, but you feel it. The emotional weight of failure is heavy and carries surreptitious baggage. Once you list out the facts on a page, your brain reads just the words on the paper, nothing else. And *that* becomes the story you are telling. That's how you make the emotional room to look for the upsides in failure.

Yes, I have made errors in life. Many, many errors. And I try to identify those and find ways to overcome them or pre-empt them next time. I want a full accounting of the reasons behind my fail-ures, but at the end of the day, I get to choose which dialogue I'm going to listen to. And what's going to be more enlightening and productive to think about? The voice that says I suck? Or the voice that says, *Try harder?*

Failure is a deeply emotional concept, but logic can be a crutch that helps us to pick ourselves back up if we use it with awareness of its pitfalls. We must stick to facts—pieces of actual truth in the proper context. What really happened during my time overseas? Once I cleared away the blinking neon sign in my brain that read, "Massive Failure," I could find my silver linings. I set out to prove a new technology, and I was successful. I have global third-party accreditation that proves my technology works. That's a logical component. No one can take that accomplishment away, and it's pretty darn good! No, it didn't even come close to my dreams for the project, but it also wasn't the massive failure that my emotions said it was. Down there, in my emotional pit, I counted my blessings. "I'm still alive, still capable, still have family and friends to turn to. No, I don't have a job, but there are things I can do."

We can perform a similar inventory after lost love. "It's true, my relationship crashed and burned. However, the fact that he/she doesn't love me any more does not mean that I'm not worthy of love. It doesn't mean I'm not the right partner for anyone...just not that particular someone." The point is you get to choose which aspects of truth you give your energy to.

You can give yourself permission to turn down the volume on the manipulative messages that originate in society and get absorbed by your psyche.

That freedom allows you to focus on the elements of your experience that will help you grow.

Remember our discussion from the Book I section, "You're being told what you need to hear"? The valuable lessons you need are out there. Your own personal "Silver Linings Playbook" should include constructive criticisms that will encourage you to grow;

guidance that can show you what specifically to do differently next time; earnest support of your value; faith in your abilities; and loving respect for your individuality. Any messages that employ shame, manipulation, embarrassment, or guilt can be summarily disregarded because you don't need that kind of "support," and it won't help you grow anyway.

Society's Role in Failure

Society is constantly pressuring us with messages that say we should be more; we should have more. It tries to tell us to avoid being frustrated, terrified, or heartbroken. Society burdens us with its demand for bravado, also known as "game face," but don't confuse stoicism with bravery. When we're at our weakest, society tells us we're less than, that this pain is our own fault, that we are inferior for feeling pain.

———

Always remember, you're in control of your own paradigm.

———

Once you're an adult, you get to decide which ingredients you build your character with. It's okay to feel frustration, fear, and heartbreak. It's okay to have weaknesses. In fact, these things are key elements of achieving greatness. Consider the people you admire, and think critically about what it is that you admire most. Is it their infallibility, or is it the grace and conviction with which they pick themselves up from failure? Do you find yourself admiring those who have never faced adversity, or those who continued to grow through struggle?

It is not true that great people never fail or never feel heartbroken. Even the world's most amazing, brilliant, successful people have weaknesses and failures. What sets them apart is that they have strategies to overcome them. I love Albert Einstein's quotation: "Do not worry about your difficulties in Mathematics. I can assure you mine are still greater." Einstein understood that admitting to and even embracing his weaknesses opened the door for growth. He also knew that he had nothing to fear from admitting his weaknesses, because he had not allowed those weaknesses to define him.

Great people know what they stink at. They can see when a situation comes along that they should ask for help with, or just acknowledge aloud that this task will be harder than other tasks. "Bear with me, this is difficult for me," they say. That magical statement gives other people the opportunity to be generous and supportive. AND it serves as a reminder to be gentle with one's self. Even just allowing yourself the room to be imperfect can make a hard situation more manageable, because you won't be worried that people are waiting for you to fail. When you make a mistake, you'll already have acknowledged that it might happen. So, no need to stand there with egg on your face. Just pick up and continue onward.

There is a huge divide between acknowledging weakness and being weak.

Great people let their strengths speak for themselves. They have a strong village, a great team. They complement one another. Most important, they accept and acknowledge their flaws, which allows them to have a strategy to be great in spite of weakness. Those who do not achieve greatness often fail because they're trying to overcompensate for the weakness. They don't want people to see it, so it becomes a bigger issue than it needs to be. They spend more energy and time covering up a flaw than it would take to acknowledge a deficit, figure out a way to compensate, and then move on. What's more, they guard this secret, and defend it with impunity. Recall our discussion on pet peeves and annoyances. When a weakness threatens our sense of worth, we become defensive.

Think again about the leaders in your life who have most inspired you. Were they perfect all the time? I'm guessing no. Sometimes the strongest position you can take is to say, "I don't know the answer, but I have an idea of how to find it." This allows you to search for help, for answers. It allows you to accept help. This potential weakness is really a potent show of strength that underlings instinctively read as authentic.

———

The strongest thing you can do is *embrace* your weaknesses.

———

But society tells us to pretend we have no flaws. In this way, our culture's messages are incorrect, even dangerous. When I dropped out of school, my fears stacked up sky high. I felt like I had let my support system down; I felt like I was taboo. Therefore, I wasn't comfortable seeking the help I needed. I understood the cultural implication to be saying that I shouldn't need any help. That I should be able to pull myself up by the bootstraps and succeed on my own. This American fairy tale about the rugged individual setting out to conquer the world is false. No one thrives without the help of others. The pressures this false paradigm of success asserts are damaging and dangerous…and exactly what we do to ourselves.

Asking for Help

Especially in time of failure there is an emotional need that must be filled, and some of that *has* to come from the outside world, though sometimes it's the last thing we want to acknowledge. When we're feeling wretched, we don't want anyone to see it. Please, hear this: accepting support is not caving to pity or sympathy.

Accepting and embracing love that is freely given is self-care.

It's like brushing your teeth for the emotional body. We think we must stand on our own and so we slough off praise; we assume kindness has an agenda or leaves a debt. Worse, knowing so intimately all of our flaws, we tell ourselves that we are frauds cleverly tricking those who would believe in us. But it's not true. Embracing the love that our village offers refills us emotionally. It builds us up when we're down. And it does the same for those who offer support. *Giving* support is just as rewarding as *receiving* it. Especially when you're in that dark spot, kindness is really hard to accept, but do it anyway.

If you are feeling like you're not worthy of accepting emotional support, it's your ego working against you again. It's telling you you're not special, which is funny because by singling you out to stand alone, your ego is setting you apart from your tribe. Likewise, in proposing that you are perpetrating the grand fraud that cultivates praise from those closest to you, you are essentially asserting that you are smarter and more clever than these people. Ironic, no? To help get your feet on solid ground in an emotional storm, you're going to need a strong foundation—you're going to need to know how valuable and deserving of love you are because so many messages you're hearing right now indicate otherwise.

How You Set Your Value Will Determine Your Fate

It cannot be overstated. The weight that your personal valuation model has on the life you are able to achieve is profound. When you catch your internal monologue using phrases like "I could never do that" or "That will never be me," guess what? You are setting yourself up to be right. In fact, thoughts such as these are the precursor to making the decision not to act. Indeed, if you do not act, you will never achieve. The cycle of personal value is self-fulfilling and can be self-defeating. If you believe something strongly enough, you will make decisions and take actions such that the realization of that belief is all but inevitable. For instance, if you believe yourself to be a businessperson with valid ideas, you will not only attend seminars and networking meetings, you will actively participate in them. You will pitch your ideas, and you will likely find others to support bringing them to fruition. Conversely, if you think, deep down, that you aren't really that smart, special, or valuable, you will skip opportunities to let your light shine. If you attend networking events at all, it will be quietly in the corner. Your big idea will not be heard, and will slowly wither away. Notice: I didn't say that if you believe in yourself, all good things will come to you. That "magical thinking" doesn't prepare you for the work necessary to actually achieve success.

Because this is so important, we need to get to the bottom of our origin stories. Where does our personal valuation model come from? Be assured that if you are not determining your own perception of value, media and society will be more than happy to determine it for you, but these influencers do not have your best interests in mind when they do. (Ahem: every successful marketing firm ever...)

What is a personal valuation model?

From my experience, a personal valuation model is the culmination of all of the elements that make up who you see when you look in the mirror, as well as the perceptions you carry regarding how others see you. That includes all of the things you do and everything that you do not do. It is the sum total of every interaction you have, and the pieces of yourself that remain after that moment. This can include insights you helped bring to light, feelings that you were a part of generating, or actual physical items that you helped to create. Where self-esteem describes how we feel about our own self-worth as a concept, personal valuation is more about how we see ourselves as a contributing member of society. It is comprised of all the unique aspects of our self that add to or detract from our influence on others.

Let me give you an example, because this is key to getting to the heart of understanding and owning your own personal valuation model. I have pretty high self-esteem. I am comfortable sharing myself with others because I believe that who I am is interesting and capable of holding up my end of a conversation. However, I place my value in the work that I do, and how I can help others. Therefore, when I am engaging in conversation with strangers, I am most comfortable talking about *them*, and my input will most naturally center around offering suggestions or anecdotes that relate dealing with similar situations to whatever they are discussing. There is very little that will offend me in most social situations. However, if anyone in the room were to cast doubt on my productivity, performance, or dedication to the things that I do, I will have a deep and instant emotional response. My personal valuation has been threatened, and my self-esteem will have almost zero weight on my perception of self in that moment. Similarly, I am not one who strives for personal accolades or awards at work. To my esteem paradigm, recognition for doing what I set out to do is embarrassing. While I always want to give my very best, I am never hard pressed to find others who are doing better. Furthermore, I am a firm believer that behind every great accomplishment is a great team, and I would always prefer to see the team be recognized. However, hearing from just one individual that something that I have done helped him or added value to his life, even for a moment; that is the most powerful recognition I could ever receive. That is where I base my personal sense of value, and I need affirmation within my value base.

A personal valuation model, then, is the system that you utilize to give all of these things weight. The weight and classification that you give to experiences, coupled with the result-versus-intention analysis (comparing what you wanted to come out of each experience against what actually did), will serve to determine the choices that you make in the future. Every decision that you make will add data to your valuation. This happens in each one of us, whether or not we are conscious about it. The benefit of a conscious exploration is that through exploration comes understanding and power. I propose that there is no greater tool to achieving mastery of your own destiny than a strong personal valuation model.

Ways in which personal valuation determines your fate:

It informs your decision making – Have you ever heard of a person taking a risk when she knew she would fail? There is an old saying that perception becomes reality, and it is true for each of us. We make decisions based on what we believe we are capable of. You cannot fail if you don't try, but you will also never know if you could have succeeded or what you would have learned along the way.

It influences who you have in your circle of friends, and the health of those connections – People are naturally inclined to gravitate toward others of like mind in social settings, and toward those who embody what we would like to achieve in professional settings. Personal valuation disparity makes for unbalanced and unhealthy relationships. For someone with a higher estimation of his personal value, there is either a drain on energy spent trying to bolster the other's low self-esteem, or a temptation to manipulate that value disparity for selfish purposes. For the person with dramatically lower personal valuation, the disparity will either be a constant oppressive reminder of his inequity, or it will provide a coattail effect allowing him to experience a sense of value inflation without overcoming the causes of his perceived low self-worth.

It determines the trajectory of your career – While there are people with low personal valuations at all levels of every business, there is a point for each of us where our career finds equilibrium. This point is determined more by our personal valuation than anything else. Skill can only get you so far. Attitude, which happens to be a direct result of your personal valuation, gets you the rest of the way. When you see people who had "so much promise" but had their career stall out, it is very likely that their abilities exceeded their personal valuation.

It defines whether or not you will be successful in your endeavors – Your muscles grow through exercise. You grow by stretching your limits, by making mistakes and learning from them. The higher your personal valuation, the more calculated risks you will be willing to take. By taking more risks that stretch your abilities and challenge your weaknesses, the wiser and more capable you will become. With wisdom and capability on your side, successes are more attainable.

———

Most importantly, belief in yourself allows you to pick yourself up when you fall, and that one thing means everything.

———

How can I take control of my personal valuation model?

Personal valuation modeling is not a course that we can elect to take in high school or college. As human beings, we are not taught how to recognize value in one another beyond the immediate "What can you do for me in this moment?" Understand that this is not entirely a mistake or oversight on the part of the architects and regents of our societal structure. A self-actualized, self-aware, and self-valuing person is, by definition, a person with true power. Insecurity, low self-esteem and misplaced self-value are all devices that can be leveraged to rob individuals of their power to make decisions and to determine their own path.

Whether or not we ever consider personal valuation, each of us has developed a personal valuation model that operates just below the surface of our consciousness in the ways described above. By making provision for our personal value, we can cultivate a healthy personal valuation model that can guide us to a more deliberate, more fulfilling, and happier life. A healthy personal valuation is the knowledge and acceptance of your strengths AND your weaknesses.

A strong and healthy personal valuation is:

Humble yet confident – I am a firm believer that you do not need to tell the world what makes you special and valuable; those are the things that you show the world through your actions and influence. Likewise, those who loudly profess their admirable characteristics usually lack them. The phrase, "I'm so generous," just doesn't fly, does it?

Supportive of others – A person who is in touch with her best and worst self knows that she cannot possibly do it alone. These people will work just as hard to bring out the best in others as they do to give the best of themselves.

Accountable – Understand that a mistake is not what defines a person's value; how you deal with that mistake is the indicator of value.

YOUR TOOLBOX:

Building a Personal Valuation Model

Developing and making positive use of a personal valuation model is a huge undertaking. It is something that you can dedicate your entire life to and barely ever scratch the surface. The only way to eat an elephant is one bite at a time, so how do we break such a huge concept into bite-sized portions? As with any exploration, it is all about asking a handful of insightful questions, answering them as honestly and completely as possible, and allowing those answers to lead you to the next questions.

The following is a list of questions I asked myself when I began my journey:

- **What do I want the world to know about me?**
- **How do I work to make it so? Is it working?**

A healthy approach to sharing your value with the world is putting yourself in positions that showcase your talents. This can be through professional, social or educational means. People with healthy personal valuation let their deeds speak for themselves. They do not seek accolades, attention or overblown recognition, although they frequently receive all of these. Defensiveness and attention seeking are typical signs of insecurity. If you find that you exhibit these attributes with respect to how you want the outside world to see you, it is a sign that you likely need to hone your craft.

- **What do I want the world to never find out about me?**
- **How do I work to make it so?**

The goal is to find acceptance in your weaknesses. Expect that everyone knows the dirty secret you have been keeping. Once you are no longer afraid of being discovered, it becomes a lot easier to turn that energy toward finding someone who can help you out with those things you aren't terribly good at. I'll let you in on a little secret: every single person who ever lived and who will ever live has something he is really bad at. Once you are open to accepting your weaknesses, you will find that others will be a lot more open with you about theirs, and often provide you with opportunities to utilize your strengths to help them.

- **Taking all of the times that I have been truly unhappy, what are the common elements?**
- **What do I believe will make me happy?**

- **Taking all of the times that I have been truly happy, what are the common elements?**

It is natural when you first ask yourself this question to think of material items or wealth. Follow this question with variations of "why?" and very quickly you will begin to discover what truly defines happiness for you. Once you know where your happiness lies, you can make decisions based on maximizing both short- and long-term happiness. These questions can provide a reality check to see if what you have just uncovered as the heart of your happiness makes sense compared to your own personal experience.

As An Aside...

Being passionate versus being driven

Passion and drive are two key adjectives used to describe success-ful leaders, but the reality is that only one of these attributes yields long-term happiness. We have all heard talk of the guy who is the first one in and the last to leave every day. That was me for most of my professional life. I would talk about working 46-hour shifts and 120-hour workweeks with a swell of pride, as though I were achiev-ing greatness through the sheer quantity of work I was willing to put in.

This attitude nearly destroyed me professionally, and serious-ly hindered my personal development.

*I was driven. People used terms like workaholic, and no life when they talked about me. While I wore these descriptions as badges of honor, it took me a great many years to realize that this form of drive was toxic to myself, **and to my professional enterprises**. What I came to recognize was that this sort of attitude was indicative of people who considered themselves driven, while those who chose to describe themselves as passionate were a great deal healthier overall. To be more specific, I came to recognize that I and the other driv-en people I knew were burning ourselves out at breakneck speeds,* whereas the passionate people were full of energy and vigor. What's more, passionate people were achieving greater results with dramatically fewer hours overall. Sure, even passionate folks put in the occasional overnighters when necessary, but they seemed to have a completely different set of rules to determine what "necessary" meant.

When I first started asking questions of people whose results and overall state of contentment were more what I was aspiring to, I was resistant to what I heard. "I'm passionate too, look at how much of myself I'm pouring into my work," I would protest. In reality, my personal valuation and insecurities were flailing to defend my fragile sense of self. It was only after I figured out how to turn down the volume of my internal defensiveness that I could begin to pay attention to what I was hearing and seeing. Here are some of the differences I have come to ascribe to the two terms:

Passion is concerned with the journey.

Drive is completely destination oriented.

This is one of the critical elements of living an inspired and inspiring life. Taking your time to enjoy the journey—to look up once in a while and see what and who is there—is essential to finding enduring fulfillment and happiness. You see, the problem with destination is that once you arrive, you have somewhere new to head toward. Because the bar will always get raised (by you), the accomplishment of each goal brings no sense of joy. There is no terminal point of arriving, other than the grave, and that is simply not the time or place to find your happiness.

Passion fills your cup, while drive empties it.

Now, let's be clear, you will always need a certain level of drive, but when it is your defining attribute, you are likely headed in a downward spiral. When you love the doing, you will be refreshed regularly through engagement with your passion. When the doing is simply a means to achieving, where do you get your recharge from?

Passion is patient.

Again, this all comes back to the journey. If you are in a hurry to reach a destination, you are likely to cut corners, sacrifice your core values and "do whatever it takes" to get things done. When the journey is your driver, you will take the time to make certain that it gets done right.

Passion loves community while drive is often selfish.

The simple fact is that, if you are a leader, very few people will share every aspect of your vision. Passionate people view that as an opportunity to get others educated and excited. Driven people view the same as a threat. Driven individuals don't have the time to waste on those who don't get it. They are too busy pushing ahead. Again, when you are driven, it is all about results, and if someone is not helping to achieve those results, they are in the way. With passion, the attention paid to the process drives the results, and mentoring along the way is a benefit rather than a hindrance.

I have always known how very fortunate I was to be doing what I love professionally, rather than holding a job. The more I learn to be passionate instead of driven, the more I am able to find success doing what I love, rather than simply pouring all of myself into my work and receiving very little of what my soul needed in return.

LOSS AND PASSION, COUSINS TO JOY

It's important, especially in times of heartbreak, to take a pause. We need to ask ourselves those questions about our happiness in order to find the upsides of what we are experiencing. Believe it or not, heartbreak has more benefit than detriments, if you can be introspective about it.

That bereft state serves a purpose. Yes, it allows time and space for grief, and that process is necessary. Heartbreak can also lead you to identify your passion centers. I can hear you saying, "Whaaat???" Yes, even if a relationship ended, even if someone was fired from a job, that's the time to look back and learn. What moments from this heartbreaking experience were joyful? What about them made you capital-H Happy? We'll circle back around to the upsides of heartbreak, but first you need to know something.

You are the architect of your own life.

You are in this space, right now, reading this book through choice. I fervently believe that people can learn to make decisions that will bring them to their best life, their highest self. Decision making has been the essence of this entire book. I want you (and me) to become more aware and deliberate about turning and twisting along life's road, instead of reacting to our subconscious triggers and the world around us.

So, we need to know what our triggers are. We need to identify and have strategies to deal with our frustrations and fears. And juxtaposed right up against heartbreak is joy. To get more of the latter with less of the former, we need to know what our deepest desires are. We need to understand what actually makes us happy. That was really my goal in writing this book; I wanted to get more in touch with the notes in my symphony that sing the sweetest, and to be deliberate about choosing them versus working my hardest on things that will invite discord into my life.

Loss

There is risk in putting your heart on the line. When you have publicly declared your goal and the process goes pear-shaped, it stinks. I'm not going to lie. However, self-protection is worse. Consider the words of Oliver Wendell Holmes who said, "Alas for those that never sing, but die with all their music in them." To live years and years, going through the motions—never getting to experience transcendent joy, only monotony—is a quiet desperation I will not endure.

The alternative, however, requires that we allow ourselves to be wrong sometimes. And that we forgive ourselves when we inevitably are. Keep in mind that it will take some false starts before you land on your happy spot.

———

Be mindful that your joy may not take on the appearance you imagined it would.

———

Especially if the process is new to you, it's common to cling to childhood dreams of your adult life's appearance, but those may be mere Halloween costumes, shells that could indicate rather than define your joy. Wanting to be a firefighter at six may demonstrate a desire to help others, but not necessarily a longing to run into burning buildings.

Coming back to the example of my alternate fuel tech project, I thought I was pouring myself into the goal of global third-party validation. Achieving that milestone was likely one of the greatest single accomplishments of my life so far, however it *barely registered* on my happiness scale. In mulling it over afterward, I realized that the magic in that dream for me was in unraveling new mysteries, engaging with experts from many industries, and collaborating in a paradigm-shifting path of discovery. That was what really got my heart pumping, and made me feel truly alive. Digging deeper, I realized that learning and teaching are two critical components of my passion center. Knowing that, in the future I can now consider new endeavors against these criteria. With a relationship, I can ask, "Is this person an active and willing participant in learning and growing?" If the answer is no, I know that the likelihood of a deeply meaningful long-term and intimate relationship is slim. It is not a judgment on the other person, just an indicator of true compatibility.

You can see that the payoffs of taking such risks are high. Though daunting, it is worth it to commit to being heartbroken. Commit to wearing your heart on your sleeve and letting people see your passions. Be willing to fail gloriously because every time you give your heart, you're not just eliminating dead-end paths. You are learning how to give your heart to something. The more you are able to identify and define your core happiness-drivers, the better suited you will be to determine which people and projects are worthy of your unmitigated passion. What's more, you will learn to have much more confidence that the object of your love will be meaningful and sustainable, which will make dropping your defenses and baring your soul much easier to do.

Learning to overcome versus moving on

One of the underlying themes of this book is learning to accept the fact that in spite of our best efforts, strategies, and plans, each and every one of us will experience and cause pain and hardships in our lives. This book is meant to help us develop methods to recognize and prepare for these hardships proactively, to face them with grace and grit, and to overcome through productive analysis and a vision of how to use what we learned to improve our future. In other words, we're learning to overcome. Overcoming differs from moving on in fundamental ways; these differences are crucial to understand and master.

The guiding principle behind moving on is to strip the offending person or event of all power, and pretend that it didn't hurt you. While I am a solid proponent of keeping your power out of the hands of those who would do you harm, there are reasons why moving on is not healthy. First and foremost, moving on as described does not have any mechanism for allowing yourself to be hurt. There is no process of internalizing, processing, and learning. There is neither the acceptance of your pain, nor the closure of growth and learning. In short, when you move on in this way, you will carry a ticking time bomb with you. Not only are you nearly guaranteed to find yourself in a position to repeat the experience by not processing the means to recognize and redirect the precursors; the pain the next time around will be magnified by the pain that you simply pushed aside the first time. Enough cycles through this, and even a small slight will produce catastrophic emotional damage.

By learning to overcome, you are committing to do the hard work just once, but doing it completely.

As you work through the phases of struggle with regard to being frustrated, terrified, and heartbroken, you will be learning the fundamentals of overcoming. It is important to validate your pain, but maintain your power. By processing in this way, you do not need to discredit the offending person or event, because you know that to do so would also discredit yourself for feeling pain. Instead, you will develop the ability to give the offense due credit without giving it your power—by recognizing that you are hurt, that the pain is justified, but that it does not have to be an encumbrance to your future. In fact, the offense can be valuable if you learn from it; you can better navigate your future.

If this is your particular story, take heart. This struggle repeats itself over and over throughout the world, even on a sociologic level. The same themes of acceptance and wrestling with ghosts of our pain are as true in cultures as they are in individuals. Those societies that declare theirs to be chosen, that cannot or will not deal with the conflicts inside their borders, are the same ones that struggle with explosions of violence from within. The lesson is this: no matter who you are, you have to deal with the conflicts and past hurts thoroughly and with intention. To ignore conflict is to invite perpetual struggle.

Making Decisions

As I began working with a team to get this book together, the question came up as to how making decisions fits in as a conclusion segment. To me, learning to understand and gain control of your decision-making process is at the heart of not only everything we have discussed so far, but of achieving a life worth living. You see, in exploring the elements of frustration, fear, and passion we are really exploring the critical elements behind our decision-making process. Without an understanding of our drivers in these areas, and a conscious strategy to increase our awareness and response to these drivers, our decisions make us.

Do you ever feel like you are barely treading water, running from one fire to the next, and never getting ahead? This is a classic sign that your decisions are making you, but not the only one. Do you know how and when to say no? Do you expect to follow through every single time you say yes? Are you noncommittal to a fault, or over-committed to the point of letting others down? As long as you are living a reactionary lifestyle, you are severely limiting the promise of achieving your potential, or fulfilling your vision of a life worth living.

So how do you go about making the transition from reactive to deliberate living? It all starts with understanding your motivations. That is where everything that we have discussed so far becomes the foundation for a more pro-active decision making process. Being aware of your default or knee-jerk reaction and the deep-rooted factors behind this reaction provides you with a better basis for understanding whether that is the best response for you. Are you playing into the emotional pressures of frustration? Are you avoiding or charging into a fear response? Are you shielding yourself from or blinded by your own passions? These are all critically informative questions to face when presented with the need to make a decision, large or small.

The next step is to measure the decision and anticipated outcomes against your core values. Exceptional leaders, and the happiest people I have ever known, are keenly aware of their core values, and use these to inform every decision they make. As you reflect on what a life worth living really means to you, you must also reflect upon what principles and values are nonnegotiable in achieving that life. Knowing your core values, and committing wholly to living them out in everything that you do, will dramatically change the paradigm by which you live your life and make decisions. Core values will help you to begin to define healthy boundaries, and boundary setting is integral to delivering on your commitments.

To be clear, this is difficult stuff, and you will have times where old habits and subconscious decision making will kick in. The key is not to beat yourself up when that happens, but to look for the trigger. Figure out what your sabotage hot buttons are, so that you can recognize when they are being pushed and catch yourself before you end up in a bad situation. The point is that as you learn to live deliberately, you will have less need to be reactive. With time and practice, you will learn to establish positive boundaries, to say no with conviction as necessary, and to stick to the things that you commit yourself to.

Choosing your battles

It's a phrase that is commonly used to remind us not to make mountains of molehills, to focus on the mountain we are climbing, not the pebbles in our paths. Yet, in this instance of my alternative fuel tech adventure, I should have chosen to battle instead of choosing my battle. What personal triggers was I succumbing to in failing to perceive the difference?

The End of a Company

"Jason, you have to look at the macro, rather than getting stuck on the micro." This remark was passed on to me by my CEO so often, it felt like a cliché. This was the response I would receive every time I was expressing our need to address what I considered a symptomatic issue with our Dutch business partner. Without fail, I would observe a statement, behavior or action of our partner that was not in alignment with our stated vision or purpose, and I demanded that my CEO and I take action. Also without fail, my CEO would proffer this nugget of wisdom followed by a soliloquy on the importance of choosing your battles. I would get infuriated by his abject dismissal of something I knew was important, and our communication would break down. Ultimately, no action would be taken, and our partner continued down the path he was headed.

After nearly four years of working together, during a summer holiday while my CEO and I were in the U.S., our Dutch business partner took actions to dissolve our partnership! I found out through a client of ours and hurried back to address whatever concerns led him to this course of action. He informed me that we suffered from "irreconcilable differences of vision" and completed the dissolution of our partnership. My CEO was baffled as to what the problem was, and declined to return to the Netherlands. How did this happen? Who was to blame? How could my partners just walk away from so much investment and opportunity?

The answer is that none of those were questions that would provide any value, nor any satisfaction. It wasn't so much a question of how this happened—I saw it coming for years—it was a question of why we, myself included, allowed it to get that far. You see, I recognized those minor infractions as symptoms of a much larger problem, but failed to convey this to my CEO in a way that was meaningful to him. I took his comment as a personal indictment rather than the clear communication that it was. He did not recognize the big picture behind why this minute issue was a problem. I did not separate the emotions from the logical component, and under the guise of "choosing my battles" I backed down from what I knew to be important. I succumbed to the battle of ego, and sacrificed our business in the process. All three of us knew long before the dissolution of our partnership that there was an underlying turbulence, but we avoided conflict, until it was irreconcilable.

YOUR TOOLBOX:

Choosing Your Battles

The concept of choosing your battles is one of those great philosophies that has been so overused as an excuse to not have the difficult conversations that it has lost all of its meaning and developmental power. As with nearly every cliché in the business world, it started out as sage wisdom, and it is that sage wisdom that I would like to tap into. As we discussed with decision making, the key is to know what the core values and long-term vision are, relevant to the issue at hand. Once those are clearly defined, the task of developing a priority scale becomes somewhat academic. Simply ask yourself the following questions:

- **Does the issue threaten core values or the long-term vision?**
- **Is that threat imminent?**

If the answer is yes to these two questions, proceed no further; this is a critical issue and it is wise to address it immediately. If the first answer is yes, but the second is no, then it is something that requires your attention, but you have some latitude to wait for the appropriate time and place. If the answer is no to both, it is not a necessary battle, and you can divert to your normal decision-making process to determine how best to proceed. It is likely that you will find that one of your frustration or fear triggers is being ignited, and the situation in question is a symptom of something else that is more deserving of your attention.

Yin and Yang of Joy and Pain

As we hinted before, there can be no joy without struggle. However, when you do allow yourself to be frustrated, terrified, and even heartbroken, the contrast of feeling when happiness returns is sweeter, deeper, and more meaningful. Being frustrated is a factor in being happy because of choice. In learning how to avoid situations that might have once sabotaged our tranquility, we can choose happiness. Amidst fearful shakeups, whether professional or personal, by keeping an eye on the ultimate goal we can aim to make the changes necessary for ultimate security. It is that element of choosing that helps us maintain a sense of control, even in chaos. By choosing to reveal the weaknesses we worry over, we get to pick what we're struggling with. So instead of working hard to cover up a deficiency or perceived lack, we instead work together with our family or team to get past a hardship. Like sweet and sour sauce, we need both positive and negative emotions to have balance in life.

Heartbreak's Key Takeaways

- Even though it's hard, risking potential heartbreak is the only way you can live the life you dream of. Committing to a deeply personal goal helps you grow and build a strong foundation. Plus, the more you experience pain, the more open you are to appreciating joy.

- Entitlement or cheating, whether in romantic relationships or personal endeavors, may look like success from the outside, but it's not. Only through complete honesty with ourselves and our partners can we know if we're even headed in the right direction.

- Heartbreak forces you to take a step back and take stock of where you are and where you have been.

- Finding your innate value amidst failure looks like knowing what value your contributions have on the world around you. How you set your personal value will determine your fate, but beware of giving your power away to others. We're not so much looking for positive opinions from others as much as we should seek to have a positive impact in our world. A healthy personal valuation is the knowledge and acceptance of our strengths AND our weaknesses.

LEARNING TO LIVE AN IMPERFECT LIFE

When I was a young professional trying to assert myself as a leader, I had absolutely no priority scale. If something was wrong, it was wrong, and everything that was wrong was a mission-critical opportunity for improvement. Imagine being one of the managers I was developing. It was a nightmare; most people tuned me out within the first couple of weeks, knowing that nothing would ever be good enough, and the rest ran themselves ragged trying to earn my approval.

One of the major problems with unscaled perfectionism (beyond the obvious fact of unattainable expectations) is an absence of scope. For me, I saw the causal dominoes from the smallest detail to the inevitable bankruptcy of a business. I did not waste anyone's time explaining why opening the restaurant with improperly set tables or burnt-out light bulbs in the dining room would lead to the restaurant going out of business. I just knew that this was the logical outcome of such complacency, obvious to anyone with eyes.

This is no exaggeration; the way I thought and acted then was frustratingly pedantic. The people I was training were justified if they determined that I was nuts. I wasn't completely off the wall; there is a logical chain of events that starts with low staff morale that can lead to a failed business. If a company fails to foster the culture of individual pride and ownership that leads to excellence in every aspect, it can and does end in bankruptcy. However, closure won't happen within a day after opening the doors with an improperly set dining room and one or two burnt-out light bulbs. These are not telltale signs that your restaurant has passed the point of no return.

———

The critical lesson that took me way too long to learn is that while every detail is important, not every dip below expectations is an emergency.

———

There are times when the show must go on, and follow-up coaching is pertinent, and other times when a change needs to be made immediately.

What I was struggling with was deeply rooted in a principle of perfectionism. I viewed the pursuit of excellence and the pursuit of perfection to be one and the same thing. What's worse is that I viewed every failure to achieve perfection or to motivate others to achieve perfection, as a failure complete. This had many undesirable consequences, including the inability to recognize accomplishments, the constant raising of the bar on myself and others to completely unattainable extremes, and the near complete surrender of my personal life to the demands of my work. I saw myself as a driven leader, but the reality was that I was driving people and my motivational influence further away. Not only was I insufferable in my standards, but I also became an increasingly worse communicator as I began to perceive questions as threats, and considered the objectives to be perfectly clear when they were anything but. I became more and more defensive as not even I was living up to my expectations, and I was always in fear of being called out or exposed.

The pursuit of perfection will invariably lead you down a path of consumption or a path of despair.

My restaurant story above is the consumptive path, where the pursuit of perfection consumes all of your energy and focus. The flip side is an overwhelming sense of despair. In both, you equate failure to achieve perfection with your being a failure, only instead of trying harder, you resign to your failure. You begin to buy into the idea that you will only continue to fail, so what's the point in trying. Either way, little by little, your ability to find purpose and happiness will fade away, and you will alienate yourself from the people who would care for and support you.

I am not going to bore you with platitudes about accepting that nobody is perfect. We have all heard it a million times, and we still can't seem to let go of this nagging feeling that anything less than perfection simply isn't good enough. Instead of telling you to accept the reality that you are imperfect, allow me to speak to this standard that we all find ourselves fixated on. For starters, let's talk a little bit about what perfection is.

Perfection Is:

Uncompromising

In order for something to be perfect, there can be no blemish, no caveat, no room for explanation or interpretation. Perfection also leaves no quarter for self-expression.

Fleeting

Perfection is a fixed point that does not stand the test of time. Changes in sociological climate and innovations continue to redefine perfection to new standards.

All Consuming

Perfection will not abide distractions or less than total commitment. Perfection is selfish and isolating, because every outside voice or perspective is a threat.

Many people get confused about the difference between striving for perfection and the pursuit of excellence. Let's look at a few key descriptors of excellence.

Excellence Is:

Engaging

Excellence is a collaborative concept, identifying the best elements of multiple influences to cultivate a sum that is greater than the parts.

Enduring

Excellence is a pursuit, and as such, it is flexible to shifting tides of discovery and expectation.

Evolving

Excellence is not afraid to fail, and is predicated on a desire for growth. Excellence does not perceive threats, merely opportunities to progress.

Now, let me ask you, which pursuit do you want to pour your life's energy into? If you forsake friends, family, hobbies, interests, and all possible distractions for the sake of achieving momentary perfection within a single finite goal, there is a chance that you will achieve it. On the other hand, if you engage with the world, open yourself to the experiences and relationships that present themselves, strive to learn and to share your wisdom with others so that they can share theirs in kind, and commit to striving for excellence in all things, you are likely to achieve more than you ever imagined.

APPENDIX

YOUR TOOLBOX STRATEGIES TEAR-OUT SHEET

Book I: Be Frustrated

Your Toolbox: Annoyance Strategy

The key to handling anything in your life that takes more than it gives is separating yourself as quickly as possible. As this relates to annoyances, this can be handled with a few easy steps:

Take a deep breath and assess the situation:

What is the cause of my agitation?

How does it impact my values, my needs or my goals?

Why am I giving it my energy and attention?

If you cannot answer the "why" question, move on and don't look back. The "what" and "how" questions will help you determine whether you are dealing with an annoyance, a pet peeve, or a genuine frustration.

Your Toolbox: Pet Peeve Strategy

What, how, and why are three of the most powerful words in our language.

To resolve my pet peeves I ask:

- What does this pet peeve represent within me?
- How did those self-perceptions get there?
- Why does this particular instance threaten my self-concept?

Book II: Be Terrified
Your Toolbox: Dealing with Advice
Ask:
What about their message hits home for me?
This question is geared toward separating out the emotional component from the logical.

How can I relate this advice to the situation?
Once the emotional bits have been separated out, the remainder is data. We are looking at the data, seeking nuggets of wisdom that we can employ as tools for current and future decision making.

How can I relate this advice to other events in my life?
This is my reminder that the tools I find are generally not disposable.

What sort of events can I project in which this information may be of benefit?
This is the future application of the history-centric application above.

How will I use this information in such future events?
This is where you internalize what the information means to you, and begin to incorporate that data into your overarching paradigm.

Your Toolbox: Decision-Making Strategy
How does this situation play into my long-term goals?
How does this situation affect the short term?
What are my emotional biases and how do they influence this situation?
What are the short- and long-term advantages of each option?
What am I giving up or sacrificing for each option?
Can I live with the consequences and opportunity cost of the decision I am about to make?

When you can answer this question with a "yes," your decision has been made. Until then, you have not completed the above. If you cannot live with the decision, there has to be a better option; perhaps you just haven't found it yet.

Your Toolbox: Response to Tangible Threats

Give it a name

The number one response that the average individual experiences in a crisis is to freeze. By giving individual problems names, our subconscious faculties can begin the organizational work that they are uniquely optimized to perform. Once the tangible threats have been identified, the rest of your strategy becomes somewhat academic.

Choose your strategy and prepare for midstream adjustments

In a tangible threat situation, everything will be new information to you. Many of our processing capabilities are referential, so with limited points of reference, you will truly be learning throughout a crisis. Being flexible to adapting will help you to recognize opportunities as they present themselves.

Know where your boundaries are and where the exits are located

Sometimes, the best option is to simply get out of there. Even if you choose or are forced to engage, identify as many ways out as you can, and ensure that your actions do not obstruct your way out.

When the coast is clear, take time to reflect

It is important to reflect on these extreme experiences while they are fresh. Take the time to embed important impressions of what triggers were impactful, and which responses achieved desired results. For the triggers where you responded undesirably, what options could have elicited more optimum outcomes?

Your Toolbox: Strategy for Taking Risks

The first step to sort out instinctive from protective fear is to ask and honestly answer a series of questions.

"What terrifies me?"

"Is this fear based on survival or ego?"

"What can I do to face this fear without sacrificing my wellbeing, or that of anyone around me?"

"What fears are most directly keeping me from doing the things that matter most to me?"

The whole point here is to eliminate nonessential and limiting fears by facing them and overcoming them. Therefore, take small steps, allow yourself to fail, and pick yourself back up and try again whenever you do.

Your Toolbox: Putting Fear Into Perspective

To gain perspective, I recommend that you write your fears down. Doing so allows you to take a step back. Distance yourself from fear and analyze the true risks here.

What if people laugh?

What if you aren't loved as much as you hoped?

What if you go your whole life without the thing you long for? What then?

Is that result really so bad, or have your goals and dreams changed as you have grown?

If the fears are indeed things you can't dismiss or let go of, are there steps you can take to mitigate the risks? Keep in mind, you can't avoid all risk.

Your Toolbox: Negotiation Strategies

My negotiation process breaks into two halves: internal and external. Of these six steps, the first three happen in my head. The last three are the conversation with the other party.

1. Removing conflict from a difference of opinion
2. Establishing a position of strength without confrontation
3. Understand what success looks like to both sides
4. Making your needs their ideas
5. Maximizing the win on both sides
6. Closing

Book III: Be Heartbroken

Your Toolbox: Building a Personal Valuation Model

How do we break such a huge concept into bite-sized portions? As with any exploration, it is all about asking a handful of insightful questions, answering them as honestly and completely as possible, and allowing those answers to lead you to the next questions.

The following is a list of questions I asked myself when I began my journey:

What do I want the world to know about me?

How do I work to make it so? Is it working?

What do I want the world to never find out about me?

How do I work to make it so?

Taking all of the times that I have been truly unhappy, what are the common elements?

What do I believe will make me happy?

Taking all of the times that I have been truly happy, what are the common elements?

Your Toolbox: Choosing Your Battles

The key is to know what the core values and long-term vision are, relevant to the issue at hand. Once those are clearly defined, the task of developing a priority scale becomes somewhat academic. Simply ask yourself the following questions:

Does the issue threaten core values or the long-term vision?

Is that threat imminent?

If the answer is yes to these two questions, proceed no further; this is a critical issue and it is wise to address it immediately. If the first answer is yes, but the second is no, then it is something that requires your attention, but you have some latitude to wait for the appropriate time and place. If the answer is no to both, it is not a necessary battle, and you can divert to your normal decision-making process to determine how best to proceed. It is likely that you will find that one of your frustration or fear triggers is being ignited, and the situation in question is a symptom of something else that is more deserving of your attention.

Make Your Own Toolbox Questions:

_____

_____

_____

_____

_____

_____

_____

_____